P9-DZZ-989

Unwrapping the Read Aloud

Making Every Read Aloud Intentional and Instructional

Lester L. Laminack

■SCHOLASTIC

New York • Toronto • London • Auckland • Sydney
Mexico City • New Delhi • Hong Kong • Buenos Aires

KH

Credits

The author and publisher wish to thank those who have generously given their permission to use borrowed material on the DVD and in the book.

Wilfrid Gordon McDonald Partridge, written by Mem Fox, illustrated by Julie Vivas (Kane/Miller Book Publishers, Inc., 1985).

Excerpts from *In November* text copyright 2000 by Cynthia Rylant, reproduced by permission Houghton Mifflin Harcourt Publishing Company.

Book cover and Illustrations from *In November* by Cynthia Rylant, illustrations © 2000 by Jill Kastner, reproduced by permission of Houghton Mifflin Harcourt Publishing Company.

Book cover and excerpts from *Roller Coaster* © 2003 by Marla Frazee. Reproduced by permission of Houghton Mifflin Harcourt.

Book cover and excerpts from *Bats* © 2000 by Gail Gibbons, reproduced by permission of Holiday House.

Book cover and excerpts from *Polar Bears* © 2002 by Gail Gibbons, reproduced by permission of Holiday House.

Book cover and excerpts from *Snow Day!* © 2007 by Lester L. Laminack with illustrations by Adam Gustavson, reproduced by permission of Peachtree Publishers.

Editor: Lois Bridges
Production editor: Amy Rowe
DVD producer: Jane Buchbinder
Video editor: Maria Lilja
Cover designer: Jay Namerow
Interior designer: Maria Lilja
Copy editor: Jennifer DePrima

ISBN-13: 978-0-545-08744-5
ISBN-10: 0-545-08744-9

9/22/09

For my sister by birth,
Amanda Jo Laminack
You were my first audience. Your delight in the stories
we shared fueled my passion for children's literature
and storytelling. You have always been, and shall
forever be, a delight in my life.

And for my sister by choice,
Reba M. Wadsworth
My dearest friend, my most trusted confidante,
my most sane advisor.

And, as always, for my son,
Zachary Seth Laminack
You have always loved a good story.
I have always, and will always, love you.

Contents

Acknowledgments

My passion for making read aloud an intentional part of the daily routine in classrooms has its origins in my childhood. I grew up in the rural South hearing stories on the porch. In my generation it was not uncommon to fill an afternoon on a porch swing with a tall glass of sweet iced tea listening to an older relative talking of days gone by. Those tales often began *"When I was your age, why, we used to...."* The language of those tales was music to my ears. Just listen: *"One time when Katie Ruth was having her a birthday party..."* and *"Did I ever tell you about the time when your momma didn't want to feed the ducks and she hit your Aunt Betty on the head with a cup? Why, she hit that girl so hard it broke that cup...."* I loved the way those stories could weave connections in my mind, drawing the relatives together into one most interesting tapestry.

I have always loved a good story—it doesn't matter if I'm hearing it or telling it. But, my fascination with read aloud was clearly shaped by baptism in the language of porch stories. The rhythms and shifts in intensity, the use of voice quality and pacing to change the tone or create a mood established a standard for what a good story should be. So it is no wonder I fell under the spell of Dr. Seuss read aloud by my brother sitting in the big chair next to my mother. It is no wonder I was entranced in the library each week by the voice of Mrs. Hand as she escorted us into the lives of Henry and Jesse and Violet and Benny. It is no wonder it became second nature for me to regale my baby sister with made-up stories and others from the books in our home. It is no wonder that I filled my own son's heart with the music of story when he was a small boy. It is no wonder that I view read aloud as a logical way of building the language and broadening the worlds of the children in my life.

So in many ways this book began decades ago. I am grateful to my family who immersed me in the language of story. I am grateful to Dr. Seuss whose playful rhythms floated on the voice of my big brother, Scott. I am grateful to Mrs. Hand who loved books and children and knew that to bring them together she had to devote time to reading aloud. I am grateful to Amanda Jo (my sister) who listened intently, shuddered at the scary parts and squealed with laughter when the story tickled our funny bones. I am grateful to my son, Zachary, who snuggled in close and asked for one more story. I am grateful to children throughout this nation who have leaned in to hear a good story come alive, and to the many, many teachers who have placed their faith in my judgment. I am grateful to the numerous conference organizers and school personnel who have invited me to speak in venues around the country as I have fine-tuned my thinking about the ways we can make read aloud a viable part of the daily lives of children.

I am grateful to Lois Bridges, my editor and very dear friend, who provides constant support and almost instant response, and who shares my hope to bring children, teachers, and literature together in a unified front to fight the erosion of the imagination.

I am grateful to Jane Buchbinder for her vision and artful work with the DVD. It was a pleasure to work with someone with an artist's soul.

I am grateful to Amy Rowe and Maria Lilja for their careful attention to detail in making the design of this book accessible and easy to manage.

I also wish to acknowledge my dear friend Reba Wadsworth for wisdom, insight, and undying support. You have seen me through the best and worst of times and remain my dearest friend. Thanks also to Lynn Daniel (TB) for believing in me in all things and for all the FD when the world begins to unravel, and to her partner, Susan West (CH), who sets me straight in the kindest of ways. Thanks to my Jubilee friends, especially Bobby, Mitch, Dean, and Lorraine, for the unconditional friendship. And finally to my good friend Joel just for being you.

Introduction

As I share read alouds with both children and teachers, I take great pleasure in bringing a book to life through the use of voice, facial expressions, and body language. The merits of the experience and the sheer pleasure of bonding with children over a book seem obvious. In fact, reading aloud to children seems as natural as inhaling and exhaling.

Yet, I have heard countless teachers express the need to justify time spent on read-aloud experiences in the instructional day. So in this book I hope to unwrap the read aloud, to reveal the gift it can be in the lives of children and the teachers who have the privilege of sharing time with them.

In my work in schools, staff development workshops, and conferences around the country, I focus on the art and function of reading aloud. I have coauthored two other books on the topic with my dear friend Reba Wadsworth, *Learning Under the Influence of Language and Literature* and *Reading Aloud Across the Curriculum*. In these two books we advocate reading aloud often and well. As I demonstrate the read aloud, I am frequently asked if I have made recordings on CD or DVD. I always acknowledge the gracious compliment but have not found a venue to deliver that request until now. *Unwrapping the Read Aloud* comes with a DVD of my work with five books as read-aloud experiences. With each of the books, I think aloud to let you see what I consider as I make decisions about how I will use my voice in the read aloud. I have selected four spreads to read aloud from each of the five books to demonstrate the significance of tone, pacing, intensity, and mood in the use of voice. In addition, the text explores the idea of making every read aloud an intentional act. That is, I focus on selecting books with great care and attention to the purpose you hold for the read aloud. I introduce this idea with an examination of three intentions for reading aloud, making careful connections to language and literacy development and to learning theory. My hope is that *Unwrapping the Read Aloud* will provide you with new options, new energy, and a new commitment to the art of read aloud and to the tremendous potential that it holds for your students.

Who Should Read This Book?

As I wrote this book, I didn't have one specific audience in mind. I thought instead of the adults who work with children and have the opportunity to read aloud to them. I thought of the children whose faces grow intense with engagement when the tension rises in a good story and whose smiles break open into a thousand bits of laughter in the funny parts. I wrote as if I were talking to the educators I work with around the country almost every week of the year. When I provide staff development or speak at a conference, I am always aware that among the folks sitting in the audience there will be classroom teachers, Title I teachers, literacy coaches, staff developers, librarians/media specialists, principals and other administrators—I wrote for them. I wrote knowing that every decision we make must be measured by the answer to one question—"Will this be good for children?" I hope as you read you will be able to say "YES!" when you are thinking about whether you should make read aloud an essential, nonnegotiable part of every single day for every single child.

Teachers

Clearly, you are the front line in the work of leading children to fall in love with language and literature as they become readers and writers. You are the ones who select the books, who set the tone of the experience, who lure children into a web of texts of all kinds. As teachers you are the daily dose of read aloud. Your voices are the ones that linger in the minds of children as they romp around on the playground, stand in line for lunch, or load onto the bus and head for home at the end of the day. You are the ones who introduce new topics and revisit favorite authors and illustrators or bring in new ones. You are the ones who deepen children's understanding of genre and open the doors to new ways of looking at life and the world around us.

Teachers, as I wrote, I envisioned you surrounded by students, captivating them with nothing more than a book and your voice. I saw your students gathered around listening intently as the tension mounted in the plot of a great story, as interesting facts unfolded in an information book, as a compelling perspective was developed in a feature article, or the details of a life were revealed in a biography. *Unwrapping the Read Aloud* is designed to deepen your understandings of the power, purpose, and art of the read-aloud experience in your classroom. The text will offer three intentions for read aloud, to inspire, to invest, and to instruct, and give you specific suggestions for living out those intentions with each read-aloud experience. In addition, there are specific connections to learning theory and to language/literacy development. On the DVD, I take five books and walk through features I consider before reading a book aloud. I selected four spreads from each book to read aloud and then come back to each spread to point out the signals or cues in the text, layout, or illustrations that influence my decisions about tone, pacing, intensity, and mood. Those signals actually make an impact on the way I use my voice in a read-aloud experience. I hope to help you notice signals like these and to use them to make each of your read-aloud experiences more robust. I imagined your viewing the DVD and then taking a few of your favorite read-aloud titles to examine carefully. Look for the signals and explore how your read-aloud performance is/can be guided by them.

Librarians and Media Specialists

Oh, you lucky people! You get to be with all the books and all the kids. What could be better? *Unwrapping the Read Aloud* offers you a means for promoting read-aloud experiences throughout the school day. The three intentions provide a framework for helping your colleagues organize and present books across the curriculum in careful, thoughtful, and purposeful ways. That gives you one more way to assist teachers in the never-ending effort to connect children and books. The DVD will heighten your attention to the design of a book and the signals the book contains to guide your use of tone, intensity, pacing, and mood when you read aloud in the library.

Literacy Coaches and Staff Developers

In your role, you have the opportunity to promote read-aloud experiences as essential instructional intentions. But as you know, talking about it, giving all the reasons for doing more, and even providing the books don't always make it the most effective experience. *Unwrapping the Read Aloud* explains how to gather a study group in a close examination of the art of reading aloud. The text and DVD will assist you in coaching your colleagues through the selection of books, articulating the intention for each read-aloud experience, and attending to the specific signals in the text. You'll have the opportunity to move through old favorites and new titles with new insights, bringing the life of the text to the surface through attention to tone, intensity, pacing, and mood.

View the DVD with your group and pause after each segment to explore new ideas in a collection of favorite read-aloud titles.

Principals and Other Administrators

Unwrapping the Read Aloud can deepen your insights into the values of read aloud in a time when there is greater attention to accountability. Use this tool to justify time spent reading aloud to children in the classrooms of your building. Use this tool to recognize the qualities of an artful, intentional, and meaningful read aloud.

Welcome, Readers

So, my fellow educators, welcome. Welcome to an exploration of the art and purpose of reading aloud. Join me in an effort to make every read-aloud experience intentional and instructional. Join me in an effort to bring read aloud back to a place of prominence in the lives of children.

A Note About the DVD

It is always helpful to see an idea demonstrated and to hear the voice of the writer, so I have selected five books to feature in the DVD. You'll see several ideas from the text put into practice. However, the most significant role of the DVD is to demonstrate how I make decisions about the tone, intensity, pacing, and mood of the read aloud from the signals in each book. While it helps to read about those ideas, it is more effective by far to see and hear them implemented. The DVD for this project has been created as a versatile tool for professional development. It is designed to allow you several options.

To anchor your reading, **view the DVD from start to finish in one sitting** as an overview of the text material in the book. As you read, return to the DVD to see examples of what you are reading about.

Organize a study group of colleagues to read the book together. After discussing sections of the text, follow up by viewing one DVD segment at a time, augmenting the discussion with a short stack of books you've collected to support the ideas in that segment. After viewing a segment, use the books you've collected to note how the delivery of the read aloud is influenced by the signals in the text.

Use the DVD segments as the focus of a study group meeting. View one segment per meeting and leave with the intention of locating books you will try out in your classroom. Begin the next meeting with the books you used and discuss what you noticed. Then move on to the next segment.

Read the book and organize a workshop to present the ideas to your colleagues, using the DVD to support and demonstrate those ideas.

Host a parent meeting with several picture books featured. View the DVD and follow up with a discussion about the importance of reading aloud to children at home. Have small groups select books from the stack to practice the power of reading aloud with attention to tone, pacing, intensity, and mood.

The DVD is divided into five sections; when you slide the DVD into your computer or play it on your TV in your DVD player, a menu with four buttons pops open on the screen. On the next page, I'll briefly explain what you'll find.

Play All

Click on this button and you can watch the entire DVD from start to finish (67 minutes).

Introduction

I provide you with an overview of the *intentional* read aloud and explain why it's at the heart of a successful classroom.

Read Alouds

Each section includes an introduction to the book, a read-aloud excerpt, and a Q&A about the process of creating an intentional and instructional read aloud. Here are the books I feature:

> *Wilfrid Gordon McDonald Partridge* by Mem Fox
>
> *Roller Coaster* by Marla Frazee
>
> *Bats* by Gail Gibbons
>
> *In November* by Cynthia Rylant
>
> *Snow Day!* by Lester Laminack

Wrap-Up

This section is a quick overview of key points.

Q&A With Lester Laminack

In this section, I answer pressing questions that address various aspects of *Unwrapping the Read Aloud*:

- Why is reading aloud so important and how do busy teachers make time for it?

- How do facial expression, body movement, and voice modulation contribute to the art of reading aloud?

- Why do students want to hear the same story over and over? When should we comply and when should we read them new works?

- What makes a read aloud *intentional*?

- Why is inspiration worthy of our instructional time?

- What makes a read aloud *instructional*?

Enjoy!

Why Read Aloud Matters

What comes to mind when you hear someone talking about read aloud? Do you flash back to your own school days and see yourself settling into your desk right after lunch? Is your head resting on your folded arms? Do you hear your teacher's voice recounting the last few events of the pages read aloud yesterday? Maybe your mind takes you to the library, that palace of books where the librarian gathered you and others near enough to get swept away in the current of language flowing on the human voice. Perhaps it isn't a school memory at all. Perhaps you are taken back even further, back to your earliest childhood memories. Does talk of read aloud evoke the smell of your mother, the tender voice of your grandmother, or the secure feeling of snuggling in close to your father? Is it a particular story or poem you recall, or is it the sound of a voice? Is it the words of the story or the cadence and the rhythm of the language? Is it the reading or the undivided attention showered upon you in those magical moments? What is it about read-aloud experiences that can leave such lasting and powerful memories long after the book is closed. . . long after. . . .

> **"As we share the words and pictures, the ideas and viewpoints, the rhythms and rhymes, the pain and comfort, and the hopes and fears and big issues of life that we encounter together in the pages of a book, we connect through minds and hearts with our children and bond closely in a secret society associated with the books we have shared. The fire of literacy is created by the emotional sparks between a child, a book, and the person reading."**
>
> —Mem Fox (2001), p. 10)

My earliest memories of read aloud take me back to an apartment over the garage behind my Grandmother Thompson's house in Heflin, Alabama. I was 4 years old. My brother Scott was 6, already in school and already reading. I remember these little boxes that came in the mail from time to time. Each box held two books, and those became instant favorites. Each night I took my perch on the wide arm of an overstuffed chair. My brother sat nestled in the seat next to Mother with the book spread across their laps. His slender fingers trailed across the page as that music—released from his mouth—lingered in the air. I basked in the glory of the rhythm, I lusted after that magic, and I coveted the nest where complete adoration flowed from mother to son. I was addicted to the whole idea of it. Of course there were others who read aloud to me. But none had the same impact in my most formative years.

But the most lasting impression of read aloud was etched into my memory in the library of Cleburne County Elementary School in Heflin, Alabama. The year was 1964. I was 8 years old, and our third-grade class made weekly visits to the library on Thursdays. I looked forward to those visits with unwrapping-a-birthday-present eagerness. I longed for Thursday, though not primarily for the opportunity to roam around the stacks of old books standing at attention, spine-to-spine with new ones. I longed for Thursday for the gift of Mrs. Hand's voice, that slow, deliberate, carefully delivered voice of books. Mrs. Hand had a distinctive voice. Low and resonant like a cello. Smooth and lush like expensive velvet. Slow and unhurried like pouring honey on a February morning. It was as if Mrs. Hand loved one thing more than sharing all those books, only one thing. Us.

> "The unique language of books and literacy is learned the way any language is learned — by using and living it as a way of life."
>
> —John Shefelbine (2004)

When she read it, was clear that she was sharing a treasure, that this was a most special once-a-week treasure that she held for us. She had such control over the elements of an artful read aloud—tone, intensity, pace, and mood. Looking back, I am convinced that my own fascination with the sounds of books read aloud—the very music of the written word played on the instrument of a well-tuned human voice—is grounded in the third-grade memories of Mrs. Hand sharing her love of books, words, and us in half-hour installments once each week.

Mrs. Hand was charged with such important duties as teaching us to use the card catalog, leading us to pledge our allegiance to the Dewey decimal system, and helping us to become adept at locating the books we needed. Although she was the undisputed queen of that palace of books, she had a deep and abiding love for reading, and, more important for us, for the children of our tiny community tucked away in rural Alabama. It was that love that guided her in the application of her knowledge. She was a wise woman and she understood something essential about becoming literate, something so obvious, yet so rare in the daily practice of our schools. Mrs. Hand understood that mastering the Dewey decimal system, becoming an ace navigator of the card catalog, and developing the ability to locate any title in less than 60 seconds would be useless skills unless we first fell in love with books. She understood that *function* precedes *form*, that the *need to know* drives learning *how to do*, that *passion* for anything is a most powerful driving force in the life of any human being.

Mrs. Hand was not wasting time reading *The Boxcar Children* aloud to our class. She didn't read those weekly installments because she had nothing else planned or because she had planned too little to fill up the time and keep us focused. She didn't read to us because she was too lazy to get off the stool. She didn't read to us because she was too unprofessional to teach us those important tools and skills of library life. She *read aloud* to us to woo us in, to seduce our minds and souls into the spell of reading. Like the call of the sirens from ancient Greece, she read to us artfully and with great intention. Mrs. Hand knew what she was doing. She read aloud to us deliberately. She selected books specifically for us, books she *knew we'd fall in love with*. She knew that once Henry and Jesse and Violet and precious little Benny found that old, abandoned boxcar, we'd be utterly and hopelessly in love. And she was right. As she read, I pictured myself romping through the pine thickets around our house and stumbling upon a boxcar. I so longed to be Henry, that brave and strong big brother who took charge and made sure all his siblings were cared for. But the truth is that I more closely identified with Benny. I was the younger brother, the weaker one, the sweet and naïve one. And when Benny found that cherished pink cup with the chip in the rim, the one his sisters scoured with a bit of soap and sand, I could taste the cold milk he drank from it. I could feel the chip as the rim touched my lips. And that was my first experience with becoming lost inside a book, falling in with and living alongside the characters. I was *forever changed* as a reader. And today, I am convinced it was in that moment that *I was born as a writer*.

Toward the Intentional Read Aloud

Let's Reclaim, Reinvigorate, Reenvision, and Reinvent the Experience of Read Aloud in Our Classrooms

There was a time when read aloud was as firmly entrenched in the daily routine of school as going to lunch. Teachers read aloud to their students with the regularity of school bells announcing the beginning of a new day. No one questioned the practice—what could possibly be wrong with something so sensible, so enjoyable, something so thoroughly satisfying as reading aloud to students. Who would dare question the motives of a teacher sitting at the front of a room on a tall stool, holding an open book while captivating the full attention of an entire classroom of children? And think of it, all this with nothing more than the human voice and well-crafted language.

Yet as I work in schools around the country, teachers report feeling they don't have time for read aloud in their increasingly busy days. They report feeling they can hardly justify time spent reading to children, and that to do so makes them feel subversive. How very sad that something so pure, something so very simple has become suspect. How very sad that we have reached a point in schooling where as teachers we feel we must justify our every decision, even the most basic, commonsense decisions about taking time to read aloud to children. So with this book and DVD project I invite you to join me in an effort to reclaim read aloud for our students and, yes, even for ourselves. Let's reinvent this tried-and-true practice, this commonsense standard in the education of our children. Let's reclaim this sensible source of endless *inspiration*. Let's reinvigorate this trusted means of *investing* in the minds of our students and opening their lives to a world beyond their own imaginations. Let's reenvision read aloud as a respected means of *instruction*. Let's make every read aloud *intentional*.

Read-aloud experiences in our classrooms:

- Serve as a foundation of a solid, thoughtful language and literacy program

- Support content in every subject area by building background knowledge that supports inquiry

- Nourish the intellect (listening comprehension is built through daily experiences hearing texts read aloud, participating in discussions of those texts, and making connections with those texts)

- Demonstrate thinking as we and our students share personal connections, make connections to other texts, take in new information, and adjust personal views

- Expand vocabulary and create sensitivity to language

- Provide exposure to text structures, helping our students understand the difference between nonfiction and fiction, poetry and prose

- Provide a demonstration of phrased, fluent reading, showing the function of tone, intensity, pacing, and mood

- Create a literary community in the classroom where a pool of shared meanings and a common language can develop

- Expand children's literary knowledge by developing their understanding of plot, character, themes, and setting

- Build a repertoire of genres, favorite authors, and favorite illustrators

- Expand our students' notions of writer's craft

To make read aloud *intentional* I believe that we must be as thoughtful in our planning as we are when selecting manipulatives for mathematics or when establishing the flow of a classroom. We must select the books we will read with the same care we take in designing centers or in setting up a science lab. We must be as diligent in considering our reasons for reading aloud as we are in selecting the focus of a mini-lesson in reading and writing workshops. In short, we must pay careful attention to our *intentions* for the read aloud. So why do we read aloud to our students? What are our expectations for the experience? What result or product do we hope for? How will our students be different for living through these experiences with us? Are we hoping to motivate them to explore a topic or genre? Are we inviting them to meet a new author or illustrator? Are we leading them to compare the organizational framework of this story with a favorite known by all? Are we simply reading today for some future benefit, investing the time now to connect future instruction later? Are we reading to introduce specific vocabulary that will be essential in understanding the concepts for a unit of study in a subject area? Are we reading to contrast the multiple meanings of troublesome words? Are we reading to raise awareness of a targeted issue? Are we reading to model a specific reading strategy or skill? Are we reading to draw them in, to lure them into wanting to read more for themselves? Are we reading to bank images and language we will draw upon in an upcoming study?

As I see it, all these *intentions* can be easily grouped under three broad reasons for reading aloud. We make read aloud intentional when we purposely select texts and times with the intent to *inspire*, *invest*, or *instruct*.

Reading Aloud to Inspire

Mrs. Hand read to my third-grade class with no other obvious intention than to captivate our hearts. She was reading to *inspire* new devotees. She wanted us to love reading, to lust after language, to crave time with books. Mrs. Hand knew we had to fall in love before we would ever see the need for strategies and skills. Remember, Mrs. Hand understood some essentials about learning. Let me quickly remind you—she understood that *function* precedes *form*, that the *need to know* drives learning *how to do*, that *passion* for anything is a most powerful driving force in the life of any human being.

Think about the teenagers you have known. One very common passion driving them, virtually *all* of them, is the vision of driving a vehicle. How is it that young people can become so enamored with the ability to drive? What plants the seed of the notion that driving is something desirable? We live in a very mobile society in which people equate mobility with freedom. From the time children are born, they are on the go. Children are strapped into car seats several times each week as the caregivers run errands, drive them to and from babysitters, daycare, school, after-school events, and more. Children see the ability to drive demonstrated over and over without explicit intentions for making them good drivers. Rather it is the mobility, the ability to accomplish so many things independently without reliance on someone else, that is the lure. I have met very few teenagers who were not absolutely *lusting* after a driver's license by the time they were 14 years old. And remember: All they have is the consistent demonstration of the *function* of this ability. Their experience with drivers is an ever-present demonstration of all the freedom this *skill* and *ability* brings with it. It takes no cajoling, no bribes, no points or pizzas. It takes little more than being witness in daily life to the *function* of the act itself.

So what can we do to create that same lusting after language, books, reading? Perhaps it is as simple as driving. We demonstrate by our daily actions the essential *functions* of reading in the life of a human being. The point here is that read-aloud experiences can be thoughtfully planned to demonstrate these functions of language to inspire our students to read and write. So each time we read aloud we demonstrate that language has purpose and power. We demonstrate that as readers and writers we strengthen our ability to use language each time we read or listen to someone else read. We put that growing strength to use each time we write and speak. As teachers, we have both the insight and the knowledge to select books carefully, thoughtfully, and purposefully. As teachers, we can decide what to feature or draw attention to as we read aloud. As teachers, we can lead our students to understand and appreciate the potentials of language that can inspire them to be readers and writers themselves. One way we do that is by being keenly aware of the functions or purposes that language serves in our lives and making those more visible for our students.

The Seven Functions of Language

Halliday (1973) identified the following seven functions of language that may help fine-tune our thinking about making our read-aloud experiences intentional.

Instrumental Language for getting things done, for satisfying one's needs

Regulatory Language for controlling the behavior of others

Interactional Language for maintaining and establishing relationships

Personal Language for expressing personality and individuality

Heuristic Language for finding things out, for exploring the environment

Imaginative Language as a means of creating a world of one's own

Representational Language for conveying information

Let's take a moment to examine each of these functions as they may relate to our intentions for reading aloud to inspire our students as readers and writers.

What the Research Says

Researchers suggest that the most valuable aspect of the read-aloud activity is that it gives children experience with decontextualized language, requiring them to make sense of ideas that are about something beyond the here and now (Cochran-Smith, 1984; Heath, 1983; Snow, 1983; Snow & Dickinson, 1991; Snow, Tabors, Nicholson, & Kurland, 1995; Beck & McKeown, 2001).

No wonder experts tell us that children need to hear a thousand stories read aloud before they begin to learn to read for themselves. A thousand! That sounds daunting. But when we do the sums, it isn't as bad as we might think. Three stories a day will deliver us a thousand stories in one year alone, let alone in the four or five years prior to school (Fox, 2001, p. 17).

Instrumental Language

The language for getting things done—instrumental—can be heard in numerous read-aloud experiences. We are witness to the use of instrumental language when a writer uses dialogue that enables a character to accomplish his or her desires and needs. If we select books thoughtfully, our students will hear the way characters use language to meet their needs, accomplish their goals, and make their wishes known each time we read aloud. As a result, we broaden our students' understandings of the potentials of both spoken and written language.

Regulatory Language

By attempting to control the behavior of others—evident in the notes and signs and warnings sprinkled throughout a book—we are using regulatory language. These may be sent by one character to another or encountered by a character in the plot of a story. Regulatory language may be sprinkled into the art as signs or labels or captions. Examples of regulatory language may also be seen in the speech of one character giving direction to another, as in *Saturdays and Teacakes* (Laminack, 2004): "My mother always said, *You stop and look both ways when you get to Chandler's. I don't care if the light is green. I'll hear about it if you don't."* We can also call attention to the use of regulatory language in situations where one character is trying to be in control. Consider *The Recess Queen* (O'Neill, 2002), when Mean Jean says, "'Say WHAT?' Mean Jean growled. 'Say WHO?' Mean Jean howled. 'Say YOU! Just who do you think you're talking to?'" These examples demonstrate for our students that language can be used to control the behaviors of others.

Interactional Language

Interactional language is used to maintain and establish relationships. We can demonstrate the function of interactional language through a read aloud of *A Letter to Amy* (Keats, 1998). Peter's letter to Amy extending an invitation to his birthday party is a clear example of written language intended to maintain a friendship. Other examples can be found in the delightful books of Alma Flor Ada, *Dear Peter Rabbit* (2006), *Yours Truly, Goldilocks* (2001), and *With Love, Little Red Hen* (2004), in which letters are sent between the characters of our favorite stories from childhood. In addition, you may find it helpful to point out incidences in other favorite read alouds where characters are using dialogue to begin or continue friendships. Each of these will be yet another demonstration of the many ways we use both oral and written language.

Personal Language

Personal language—used to express personality or individuality—can be found in most any read aloud in which the writer reveals a character through playful word choice. Junie B. Jones, the spirited young character featured by Barbara Parks in numerous books, comes to mind as a good example of a character whose language is part of her personality. You will find similar examples in the Amelia Bedelia books created by Peggy Parish. For other examples of personal language, share Helen Lester's *Hooway for Wodney Wat*, or Roald Dahl's *The BFG*, or Judy Blume's books featuring the effervescent younger brother, Fudge. In each case, the writer's choice of language for these characters etches a lasting memory in the mind of the reader and listener.

Heuristic Language

Heuristic language, used for finding things out or for exploring the environment, is quite common in classrooms. Heuristic language can be heard in the hundreds of questions asked each day in a typical classroom. We can also see it in the all-about and how-to books and the information books in our nonfiction collections. We can feature this use of language through read-aloud experiences with selections from Gail Gibbons, Cathryn Sill, Seymour Simon, Diane Siebert, Nicola Davies, and Thomas Locker. Many of our favorite nonfiction writers will give us ample opportunity to use language to find out and explore.

Imaginative Language

The language of the imagination is used to create a world of one's own. Young children seem quite comfortable with pretending and talking about things and situations as if they were real. They create towns with blocks, go grocery shopping in the dramatic play areas of their classrooms, and travel to the moon just by climbing up a ladder. Each time we read aloud a book in which the author takes us on a journey of suspended logic—where we imagine and pretend—we are wallowing in imaginative language. So when the children in *Roxaboxen* (McLerran, 2004) create a town using rocks to outline the buildings and create their own rules and government and currency, they use imaginative language. They talk about imaginary things as if they were real. Through books such as this we help our students see imaginative language at work. Clearly, then, any work of fantasy, folktale, or fairy tale capable of evoking the imagination can be read aloud, showing yet another function for both written and oral language.

Representational Language

For a striking example of representational language, take a look at *The Handmade Alphabet* by Laura Rankin, in which sign language is demonstrated in beautiful language and art. The National Council of Teachers of English's Orbis Pictus Awards are a good source of outstanding books that convey facts and information. (See www.ncte.org/elem/awards/orbispictus.)

How to Select the Perfect Read Aloud

So it seems quite simple, really. If we want to make these seven functions more visible we need to read to them. *Read aloud* to them. Don't just pick up a book at random when there are a few extra moments at the end of a science lesson—take the time to carefully select what we read and think deeply about why we are reading it. This seems like such common sense, doesn't it? If we want children to *desire* the ability to read, we *inspire* them by inviting them in. We read to them, showing our sheer delight in the act of reading. We read to them, letting them hear the sound effects in the background of our minds, the voices of the characters lifting up off the pages, the very mood of the text in the tone and intensity of our voices. We control the most basic elements of a read aloud with our human voice—tone, pacing, intensity, and mood. We let our children live alongside characters in books. We let them investigate the habitats of polar bears and explore hot, dry desert terrain. We let them stand alongside children facing bigotry in the Jim Crow South. We let them know the sting of bullies. We let them know the strength of standing tall and facing a challenge. We take them into the celebrations of another culture. We let them laugh with delight at the antics of a favorite character. We show them two perspectives on the same news event. We lead a great discussion as a reaction to a letter to the editor. We launch a new study from the questions raised by responses to a book on bats. We read to them. *We read aloud to them*, and we do so with carefully thought-out *intentions*. We let them see, experience, live through the freedoms and thrills and satisfaction a reading life can provide.

When we read aloud to inspire, our expectations of students are simple and direct. We want nothing more than to pique their interest, to spark a desire, to entice them to read. Our ultimate goal is that they fall in love with language and books, that they lust after language and books and reading as they will later lust after driving. Therefore, any intentional read aloud designed to inspire would not ask students to answer a set of questions, give a retelling, unpack meaning, host a conversation, define vocabulary, write a character sketch, compare or contrast anything. None of that would follow a read aloud to inspire our students. Rather, we want to leave them laughing. We want to see their eyes welling up with tears in those poignant moments in the text. We want them holding their breath as suspense builds. We want to leave them begging: "One more book...," "Five more pages...," "Just one more paragraph, please, we have to know what happens...." We want them talking about the book as they are walking to lunch, scurrying about on the playground, boarding the bus. We want the language lingering in their heads. We want the reading to have lasting power. We want them to want reading for themselves.

So when we read aloud with the intention to inspire, we will naturally rely on favorite authors and beloved titles that we have fallen in love with over and over. One thing is sure here: Our passion and zeal for the act of reading and for the material being read must be evident. Then we move on to introduce our students to new authors and illustrators, broadening the set of options, widening the net for matchmaking, so to speak. We are careful to introduce new genres and expose our students to a range of topics. We select material for read-aloud experiences knowing that our students have varied interests and backgrounds that will influence their attractions to reading. When reading aloud with the intention to inspire, we may select a short poem about baseball, a feature article about chameleons, or a letter to the editor protesting a plan to clear the woods behind the school to make a space for a fast-food restaurant. We may select a chapter book that will be shared in several installments across two weeks. We may select student-authored material or perhaps something we have written. We may select a collection of riddles and jokes. We may select a set of stories about school. The point is, we select *what* we read with the same intentionality we follow in selecting *why* we read. In fact, *what* we read aloud is inextricably connected to *why* we read aloud.

Know Your Students, Know Authors and Illustrators

It seems obvious, then, that as teachers we must fine-tune our knowledge in two essential areas. The first is knowing our students as humans—knowing where their passions lie. Knowing what they value, what they hope for, what they fear. Knowing what they love and hate. We must know the very essence of our students if we are to stand a chance of having what we read resonate with their being, if we are intending to inspire them to read and write. Beyond that, we must know books and stories, articles, and poems. We must know authors and illustrators. We must walk with bookshelves in our minds and stand ready to pull the next book when the opportunity presents itself. We select a particular title for a read aloud because we know it:

- Promises to be enjoyable for our students—it holds the potential to excite, move, entice, delight

- Connects to an aspect of our curriculum—the text has clear links to social studies, science, math, music, art, language arts

- Highlights the music of language and offers opportunities to model fluent reading, phrasing, and well-crafted writing

- Contributes to an author study—it gives us a chance to zero in on a particular author's writing style, focus, themes, and topics

- Highlights key literary elements or provides good demonstration of particular text structures

- Addresses important issues like friendship, racism, competition, or peer pressure

- Presents multiple perspectives—consider global literature across time and culture

The Importance of Timing

The timing of a read aloud is another critical factor for consideration. If we want this read aloud to inspire children to pick up a book, to explore new authors and genres and topics, we need to make it a standard feature in the daily happenings. When this read aloud occurs daily at a specified time, children will begin to anticipate the moment. They will watch for the signals demonstrated in your actions as you move toward the basket of books you selected to read this week. They will keep their eyes focused and settle in to hear what you are about to present. The read aloud becomes a ritual, a part of the daily routine that helps them mark the passage of time and live with a sense of focus and expectation.

Reading Aloud as an Opportunity to Invest Our Time in Developing Language and Concepts

When we *invest* in anything we expect to make small installments over long periods of time with the understanding that dividends will not be collected until much later. Talk with anyone nearing retirement and they will tell you how very important it is to make contributions of any size as often as possible to the general fund.

> "Powerful writers and powerful speakers have two wells they can draw on for that power: one is the well of rhythm; the other is the well of vocabulary. But vocabulary and a sense of rhythm are almost impossible to 'teach' in the narrow sense of the word. So how are children to develop a sense of rhythm or a wide vocabulary? By being read to, aloud, a lot!"
>
> —Mem Fox (1993, p. 68)

Retirement age is too late to begin thinking about what we *could* have done or *might* have done or *should* have done to live well in our later years.

Likewise, if *investment* is the specific intention of a read aloud, then we select books for the potential each of them holds. We think in advance of the outcome or product we desire. So with that in mind we begin with a close look at the specific subject and the unit of study. We identify the core understandings needed for successful completion and select books that will enable us to create scaffolds through exposure to images, specific vocabulary, and concepts that new learning can be built upon. We sequence these texts both in a way that will be logical for the learners and will scaffold the concepts in the study.

Then, in careful, thoughtfully planned, and patient installments we layer each read aloud to establish a collective common ground of the classroom community, and we pace the presentation of texts to the ability of our students to process the essential information. The main point here is to *invest* the time *now* to read aloud from these specifically selected texts with the expressed intention that the time spent now will yield significant dividends during the actual study as it unfolds. Think of it this way: Time spent reading aloud on this end helps to establish the common ground that you connect with comfortably as you begin the more in-depth work of the unit of study. For a detailed listing of books carefully selected to support read alouds intended to *invest* time, language, and concepts, see *Reading Aloud Across the Curriculum* (Laminack & Wadsworth, 2006).

> **"Reading aloud is not a cure-all. Not quite. But it is such a wonderful antidote for turning on turned-off readers and brightening up dull writing that I feel it's worthwhile to plead again for its regular occurrence in every classroom, not only those classrooms at the younger end of school. . . . The value of my writing increases before my very eye, beneath my very pen. The investment in *listening*, I have found, pays dividends."**
>
> —Mem Fox (1993, p. 70)

Investing Time, Language, and Concepts

When we gather books for reading aloud to invest time, language, and conceptual information, we group them around the following:

Author study A collection of books written by one author selected for a close examination of the writer's style.

Genre A collection of books from the same genre selected to explore the parameters of the genre. This may lead into a unit of study in writing workshop or reading workshop.

Text structure A collection of books selected to demonstrate one or more ways of organizing texts or to demonstrate selected craft techniques in writing.

Topic A collection of books selected to establish background, build vocabulary, develop concepts, or otherwise create a framework for deeper study of a specific topic, such as the Underground Railroad, the water cycle, or bats.

Theme A collection of books selected to broaden or deepen an understanding of a selected theme, such as friendship, community, bullying, and so on.

TEACHING TUTORIAL I

Using Literary Concepts to Group Books

1. Genre
2. Theme
3. Topic

Genre

As I explain these literary concepts to students, this is what I say: "Let's think for a moment about pets. When we talk about pets, people often ask, 'What kind of pet do you have?' And of course we tell them. We may say, 'Oh, I have a dog, and his name is Oliver.' Or we may say, 'My pet is a kitten. I got her at the animal shelter, and she is orange and white and fluffy and she has little white tips on her tail and her ears.' We might answer that we have a fish or a gerbil or perhaps a bird. Well, when we choose books to read someone may ask, 'What kind of books do you like?' To answer that question it helps to know about the kinds of books we can find. We know about kinds of pets like cats, dogs, birds, fish, and others. Well, there are different kinds of books also, like fables and folklore and fairy tales. There are mysteries and adventures and historical fiction. There is poetry. There are nonfiction information books or all-about books or essays. Oh, there are so many kinds of texts to read and write, and *genre* is the word we use to talk about what kind of book or text it is. So this week I am going to read aloud five books from the same genre."

Theme

"Take a look at this [show a bumper sticker with a message you can explain, for example, "Think Global, Act Local" or "Love Your Mother," followed by arms hugging the globe]. We usually see bumper stickers like these on cars. A bumper sticker is a short way to give a big message—also known as *theme*. Think about the big message or theme in these two bumper stickers. We could put those bumper stickers on a bucket and fill the bucket with books and articles and Web sites and poems and essays about ways to help take care of Earth, ways that we could help in our own homes and in our neighborhoods and towns.

Today we are going to write a bumper sticker to help organize some of our books. We can begin by thinking about the book I read aloud to you this morning. The title was *Stand Tall, Molly Lou Melon* by Patty Lovell, with illustrations by David Catrow. In that book, Molly Lou was shorter than her dog and her teeth stuck out so far she could stack pennies on them. Her voice sounded like a bullfrog and she was fumble-fingered. There were many things other people might tease her for. But she didn't mind. She never let any of those things bother her. And remember how her grandma kept telling her something. That helped her to be strong. I'm going to read this book again, and this time when we finish I'd like you to try writing a bumper sticker that gives the big idea in just a few words. [When you finish the book give them a brief time to work in small groups of three or four to make a bumper sticker. You may find it helpful to have strips of paper cut into the shape of an actual bumper sticker. When they finish, have them share with the class to hear the different ways the basic theme can be expressed.] Now let's see if we can take these and come up with one way to identify the theme and tell the big idea here.

Tomorrow we are going to try stretching our thinking a bit. I'm going to bring in a few books we have heard before. We will pause for a moment after I read each one and talk about whether the book belongs in our bucket or not. We want to include only those books that would have the same bumper sticker or theme."

Here are a few titles to begin with:

- *Dumpy La Rue* by Elizabeth Winthrop
- *Odd Velvet* by Mary L. Whitcomb
- *The Sissy Duckling* by Harvey Fierstein
- *Dog Eared* by Amanda Harvey
- *Ira Sleeps Over* by Bernard Waber

Topic

"Let's think about a time when there was big news in our class. Try to remember that time a bird flew into the lunchroom. Remember how it fluttered all around, trying to get out? That poor little bird was so frightened. Do you remember how kids and teachers were going nuts? Do you remember how Mrs. Freeman in the lunchroom was able to get the bird to fly out the big doors leading to the parking lot? Wow, that was a crazy day! But what I remember most about that day is how everyone in the whole school talked about that bird for days. Yes, I remember how that was all anyone wanted to talk about. The bird in the lunchroom was the topic of almost every conversation. Well, sometimes we choose books about a topic. So this week I am going to read aloud five books about bats. Each day I'll read one book about bats, and by the end of the week we will know much, much more about bats than we do today. Our topic for this week will be bats. Let's begin with this book. . . ."

So let's think about how we might introduce each cluster of books to children.

Author Study

"Today I'm going to begin the books collected in the white basket. Each of these five books is written by one of my favorite authors, Mem Fox. Each day I will read one book aloud for you. I want us to begin thinking about the way Mem Fox tells a story. Let's see if we can notice those things Mem Fox does really well as a writer and storyteller."

Genre Study

"You may have noticed that as I have read books to the class I sometimes put them in this white basket. The books I've collected for this basket are together because each of them is a very good example of a memoir. Tomorrow we will take these five books from the basket and talk through what we remember about each one. As we do that, I'd like you to think about what these five books have in common, what makes them belong together in one basket. Then I'll read the books again so we can decide what makes a good memoir."

Text Structure

"I've pulled together a set of books to read this week. We have read each one before so I'm sure you will remember the story as soon as you see the cover. The reason I put these books together is that each one shows us a different way to move the story forward. So now I'll show the cover of each book and read the title, author, and illustrator. As we read them aloud over the next few days, we will make a chart of all the ways we know a story can be organized and can move from start to finish."

Topic

"As you know, we will begin a study of bats next week, so I've searched through the books we have in our room and in the school library. I've pulled together a set of books that will help us learn some of the vocabulary we will need to talk about bats. I was also careful to include books that have very good illustrations that will help us know what we are talking about. As we read these books this week, we will be able to ask even better questions and learn much more about bats in our science unit."

By way of example, let's assume you are going to study bats in your science curriculum. You might use the following set of books to build background:

- *Bat Loves the Night* by Nicola Davies

- *Bats* by Gail Gibbons

- *Bats* (Let's Investigate series) by Nancy J. Shaw

- *Bats* (Animals, Animals series) by Margaret Dornfeld

I would read these books in this order to create a slow accumulation of information. In this order, the set moves from least complex to most complex. The level of specificity increases from book to book, and the text features become more complex. We will explore the use of a set of books like this in more detail in a section called Making Read Aloud Intentional: One Possibility (see page 52).

Theme

"We have been having community meetings about creating a safe school, and some of our discussions have been about taunting and teasing and bullying. Well, I have collected a group of books that will help us think more about that. As we read these books I'd like you all to think about a few ideas: What can we do if someone is taunting or teasing or bullying one of our friends? What makes someone be a bully? What should you do if someone is taunting, teasing, or bullying you?"

What the Research Says

Trade books are superb sources of vocabulary. From 80 books (40 targeted to kindergarten and another set of 40 targeted to first grade), we identified about 1,500 words that could be taught to children (Beck & McKeown, 2001).

Teaching Tutorial

Revisiting/Rereading of Texts

When we read aloud to our students with the intention of making an investment in future learning, we are spending the time to select and read material today with the purpose of layering in concepts, images, and vocabulary that we will revisit in the days or weeks to come. Think of this as laying a foundation for future teaching. For example we may read today from Thomas Locker's *Water Dance*, knowing that next week we will anchor a mini-lesson for the writing workshop featuring the poetic structure in an informative text. At that time, we may revisit a Diane Siebert book such as *Mississippi* to show another example of a poetic structure for a nonfiction text with a related focus. And later in that same week, we may return to both of these books as the common ground for our work on the water cycle in science. Locker's poetic structure for a nonfiction project could be a model several students want to try out. At the same time, we can make clear and tangible connections to the phases of the water cycle with the various perspectives the water speaks from in Locker's short and beautifully illustrated book. We may also choose to revisit the poetic, first-person voice of the river in *Mississippi* to see the impact of humans on the groundwater. In any case, when we read to *invest*, we are careful to point out specific details, vocabulary, images, and ideas we want our students to notice and return to later. We point these out in the moment of reading to call attention to them, not to pause and unpack the ideas or develop the concept. In this first reading, we are establishing a base layer—an investment toward future instruction—that we will return to and build upon when we are into the unit of study at the point of direct instruction.

When we read aloud with the intention to invest our time, those intentions not only influence the decisions we make about what to read, they also influence the decisions we make regarding delivery. First, we know that investments are made over time, so we plan to read these texts over time, not just once. Short texts such as picture books, poems, articles, and essays are most likely to be read several times each. In fact, over the course of a unit of study, a single text of this type may be read as a whole (or in revisited parts) several different times as you lead up to the study you are scaffolding for. For longer texts such as information books (e.g., Seymour Simon), chapter books, and reference materials could be read in installments. The idea here is to make small deposits, layering one upon another as you work toward significant holdings that will have the necessary substance and volume to become the core that curriculum and instruction can build upon. In this way, we establish some common ground for each learner in the "investment pool" and increase the chances of a more substantial yield at the conclusion of the unit.

In addition, we model the strategies useful to building background needed for a deeper study. We demonstrate that learning is a layering process much like that which forms hailstones. Think about moisture collecting in the atmosphere, gathering and accumulating mass until it begins to fall. As these accumulations of mass (hailstones) fall through the atmosphere, they get caught up in thermal updrafts that toss them back into the cooler moist air, recoating the hailstones and creating greater mass, volume, and weight. This may continue over and over until the hailstones are too heavy for the warmer air to toss back up. The result is, of course, a hailstorm.

In much the same way, a read aloud intended to invest layers images and ideas, information and vocabulary over time. Each read-aloud experience layers new mass, new volume, new weight, giving students more to think about, more to think with, more background that will help them fine-tune questions and build a more solid conceptual foundation. As teachers, we recognize that children often gather words before they have a full grasp of the concepts and big ideas associated with or represented by those words. This layering process, grouping books to be read over time, is an investment in the development of vocabulary and conceptual background. All this accumulation makes each subsequent experience more robust and leads eventually to a "hailstorm" of knowledge.

Each time we read aloud with the intention to invest in our students' developing understandings, we are making a statement about learning. This practice assumes that learning takes place all the time, and over time, that learning is something that layers and connects. It assumes that learning is a rather natural process. Frank Smith (1998, p. 3) contends that "we learn from the people around us with whom we identify. We can't help learning from them, and we learn without knowing that we are learning." So think about the time we spend reading aloud to invest. Think about the learning that is taking place as we form a community of influential people—a community that includes our students, ourselves, the writers whose work we feature, and the characters or information captured in their work. Smith (1998, p. 11) refers to communities of influential people as *clubs*. These may sometimes be the formal organizations that we join and maintain membership in. But clubs may often be the informal associations that we belong to just by sharing an interest and a sense of community. . . all of the different groups with which we identify. And as we identify with other members of all the clubs to which we belong, so we learn to be like those other members. We become like the company we keep, exhibiting this identity in the way we talk, dress, and ornament ourselves, and in many other ways. The identification creates the possibility of learning. All learning pivots on who we think we are, and who we see ourselves as capable of becoming.

When we devote time to read aloud as a regular and consistent part of our classroom routine, we create a community of influential people, a club of sorts. As the reader, the voice of the music in language, you become *the* influential person in this new club. The fact that you spend valuable time each day to read aloud sets a standard for the club. The fact that you read books to layer learning, to build vocabulary, to develop an image bank also sets a standard in the club.

Smith (1998, pp. 11–12) further contends *[a] remarkable characteristic of the learning we do from the company we keep, effortlessly and inconspicuously, is that it is vicarious. We don't have to do anything ourselves in order to learn except put ourselves in the company of people with whom we identify. Other people do things, and we learn. We don't learn as a consequence of what other people do; we learn at the moment they do things—always provided that we see ourselves as members of the club. It is trial and error learning, if you like, but since the trial is performed by the experienced person who will be learned from, not by the inexperienced learner, there is rarely error.* So as we read today with intentions for investment in future learning, the members of our "club" are learning all along, each moment of each read aloud.

Brief Pauses to Call Attention to Language

1. Luscious Language
2. Interesting Language Play
3. Intriguing Words
4. Made-Up Words

Luscious Language

When reading *Saturdays and Teacakes* by Lester Laminack I would pause after these words—**"In Mammaw's big kitchen, sunlight poured through the windows like a waterfall and spilled over the countertops, pooling up on the checkerboard floor."** Just as I finished the last word in that sentence I would pause, look at the book, then at the students and say something like: "Wow, can't you just see the sun coming into that kitchen? It isn't like the whole kitchen is filled with sunlight, it's just one window the light is coming through. Lester sees the light like a waterfall coming through the window. That's such an interesting image and it helps me think about how the light looks in there. Let's read that once more..." At this point I'd read that sentence again and then continue reading. The point here is to call attention to specific language, to bring it to their conscious awareness. You can return to that at any time in the future with various intentions, but here we simply want to lift it out briefly, admire it, make a small comment that gives it value, and move on.

Interesting Language Play

When reading *Snow Day!* by Lester Laminack for a second or third time I may pause after reading the spread with this language—**"Yippee! Wonderful, amazing, we-can't-go snow."** Just as I complete the page I stop briefly and

Teaching Tutorial

say something like: "Have you noticed that when I read that line I always say 'we can't go' very quickly? Let me show you what Lester has done here. Take a look at this page. See how he writes those three words; he places a dash between each word. That sort of links them together like a chain. It kind of makes it one word instead of three, and that's why I always say them very quickly." Then I move along and continue reading. I would pause like this no more than one or two times in any one reading of the book.

Intriguing Words

When reading *Bat Loves the Night* by Nicola Davies I would pause after this sentence—"She unfurls her wings, made of skin so fine the finger bones inside show through." As I read the last word in that sentence aloud I'd pause, point to the illustration with the unfurled wings, and say something like: "*Unfurl.* Isn't that an interesting word? I don't think we have heard that word in any other book we have read. *Unfurl.* Notice in the illustration how bat's wings are now spread out. *Unfurl* means to open or unfold. Notice how the bat's wings are folded in, tucked close to her body in these illustrations [on the left side of the same spread]. And now in this illustration she has them open, unfolded. She unfurls her wings." [I frequently fold my arms in close to my torso and then demonstrate the act of unfurling with my arms.] Do this briefly, call attention to the word, and say it a few times so it resonates in their ears. Link it to the illustrations, offer a definition in the context of the information, demonstrate the meaning, but do something to lift it a bit. I would do this in only one or two places as I read through. Remember you can reread any book, and with each "visit" to the text you can make new discoveries.

Made-Up Words

When reading Sheri Bell-Rehwoldt's *You Think It's Easy Being the Tooth Fairy?* I'd pause after reading this segment— "And I'm SMART! Take my amazing Tooth-o-Finder, for example. I invented it." After reading that bit of text I'd pause and point to the illustration of the watch-like apparatus on her arm and say something like: "Did you hear what she called this? [pointing to the device] Tooth-o-finder. Isn't that fun? She just made that up but it makes sense, doesn't it? It's like an invention. The character invented this [again point to the illustration of the device], and the writer invented a name for it. How fun!"

That's about all I'd do with it. Just make them aware of the way writers can play with language with purpose.

Reading Aloud to Instruct

When we set out to instruct another person, there is typically a relationship established that defines our role. The instructor is assumed to be competent, masterful, accomplished, and perhaps even artful in something that the apprentice or student *needs* or *wants* to learn. But as teachers, our work is done in an institution of learning where student attendance is mandatory. Our students are not seeking us out because of our passion and competence, or because of our accomplishments or our artful application of knowledge and skill. Our students aren't even selecting to be in our specific classrooms. Their choices are limited from the start. It isn't their drive to know, their passion for a topic, that sends them out on a mission to find a mentor. So we can't assume that all of our students are eager to learn what we have been charged to teach.

Let's explore how a read aloud intended to instruct can be a most beneficial experience in this situation. Assume for a moment that your students are expected to study mammals in science, more specifically, bats. Let's further assume that the curriculum expects your students to be able to compare and contrast the bone structure of a bat's wing with the bone structure of the human arm and hand. Let's also assume that your students are expected to explain echolocation, nocturnal behavior, the dietary habits of bats, bat habitats, and care and feeding of their young, and to be able to discuss and debunk common myths and misconceptions regarding bats.

One way this might be approached is through having students read traditional science textbooks, answer questions that are either teacher-generated or found at the end of chapter sections, write definitions for vocabulary words using the glossary, locate specific information using the index and/or table of contents, make a model, draw a diagram, and so on. Much of this might be done as classwork and would make extensive use of the textbook as a primary source of information. Clearly, most teachers are adept at extending this sort of instruction with interesting inquiry projects, research projects, field trips, guest speakers, and the like, that can be layered in to make the project more engaging. However, the background each student brings to the textbook will be limited and uneven. As the study begins, some will read through the assigned material (perhaps more than once), noting only what is specifically asked for in the questions at the end of the chapter. Perhaps they will take note of the words in bold or italics that are keyed to the glossary. It is also quite possible that students may become quite adept at matching statements from the text with questions from the end of the chapter (i.e., finding the correct answer). It is possible, then, to "do well" in school without actually learning anything about the topic. In short, the event becomes an exercise in assembling a puzzle in which the reader seeks out pieces from the questions that fit together with pieces from the text; it's something of a matching game where the task is to find the interrogative form at the end of the chapter and match it to the statement form within the chapter. Making the correct match doesn't prove understanding.

If we follow Frank Smith's idea that learning is natural, that we learn from the company we keep, then what does that suggest for us about reading aloud with intentions to instruct? Can we actually read aloud as instruction? Yes, we can.

The key, as I see it, lies in our intentions. If we intend to instruct through the read-aloud experience, then much rests on the sense of community we have established and on the very careful selection of books. As with any intentional instruction, we must know what we expect our students to learn as a result of the experience. We begin with those expectations, and we place them alongside our knowledge of our students. We assess their existing background knowledge, including their current insights and misunderstandings. Through initial conversations, we determine their facility with vocabulary related to the topic and their ability to speak with specificity using that vocabulary. These insights aid us in selecting books to read aloud and also serve as common ground for developing and extending communal concepts about this topic.

Brief Instructional Pauses to Call Attention to Concepts or Content

1. Pronunciation Guides and Captions

2. Defining Vocabulary in the Text

3. Layering Ideas

Pronunciation Guides and Captions

When reading *Snakes* by Gail Gibbons stop after you read page 5—"Herpetologists (her-peh-TOL a-jists) have identified about 3,000 different kinds of snakes in the world." On this page there are two important features included to assist the reader. Call attention to the pronunciation guide included in parentheses for the word *herpetologists*. Also point out that the illustration depicts a group of herpetologists at work and includes a caption that defines the word. So as I read to the end of the page I may say something like:

"*Herpetologists*—that is an unusual word. We don't see that one every day, do we? Did you notice the way Gail Gibbons helped me know how to say that word? Let's have a look at the support she put right in the text [point to pronunciation guide in parentheses]. See how she breaks the word into syllables for us and spells each syllable the way it sounds? It is just the way it's done in the dictionary. That lets us know how we should pronounce the word. Notice that one syllable is in capital letters. That lets us know which syllable is stressed, or gets the most 'punch' when we say the word. [Say the word without the stress on -TOL- and again with that syllable stressed to demonstrate the difference in sound.] And there is something else I'd like you to notice in this illustration. She includes captions in the art to give us additional information. Notice the word *herpetologists* written between the man on the left with the pointer and the woman on the right making notes on a pad. Let's read the caption—

'Herpetologists are scientists who study snakes.' Now we even know what this big new word means. We know that a person who studies snakes is called a herpetologist."

I would not do this with each page, and I would not do this on the first read aloud of the book. In my opinion, to do both would take away the freshness of exposure to the information. Read the book once all the way through, build excitement about the topic, spark interest, and generate questions. You'll have ample opportunity to revisit the book. On each revisit you can select one or two features to layer into the repertoire. And, of course, there are several other features of nonfiction that you could and should highlight.

Defining Vocabulary in the Text

When reading *Polar Bears* by Gail Gibbons I would pause after reading the spread with these words—"The polar bear lives in the Arctic, the area that surrounds the North Pole. Part of the Arctic is frozen, treeless land called tundra. Most of the Arctic is ocean. Ice covers the water most of the year."

Here I would say something like this: "Let's take a moment to think about what Gail Gibbons is doing here. Notice she is giving us two new words—*Arctic* and *tundra*. Let's read this page again and this time notice how she tells us what tundra is. [Read the page once more, slowing down on the embedded definition of *tundra*.] In this sentence—'Part of the Arctic is frozen, treeless land called tundras.' —she gives us the definition and the word. Writers often do that when writing nonfiction. I noticed she also helps us with knowing where the Arctic is and what that area is like. Let's look back to the text and make a list: ARCTIC = (1) land that surrounds the North Pole; (2) part is frozen tundra; (3) most is ocean; and (4) ice covers the water most of the year. Wow, just look at all that Gail Gibbons layers into this one small page. So when we read nonfiction, it helps to read it once to get the big idea of the information and then read it again carefully, noticing how the writer helps us make sense of new ideas and new words."

Again, I would not go to this extent with every page, and I would not do this more than once or twice in a single visit to the book. However, if you have read this book several times it could be interesting to explore each page as a nonfiction investigator searching for the supports she includes for her readers. That could only strengthen them as readers and as writers of nonfiction.

Layering Ideas

When reading *Bat Loves the Night* by Nicola Davies, I notice that pages 6–7 have about six ideas layered into the 39 words of the main text on the spread. An additional three to four ideas are introduced in the smaller text surrounding the larger illustration on the right page of the spread. I also notice that the text is organized into six segments strategically placed around the four illustrations on the spread. As I read this to children I always slow the pace and allow a bit of extra silent space here to let the separate ideas settle. As I draw the two pages to closure I stop and say something like:

"Take a look at this. Nicola Davies has smaller words in italics over here [point to the smaller italicized print]. Writers do this to give us extra information. Sometimes it is helpful to read these when you come to them and sometimes it may be just as well to read them after you have read the whole book. Let's try reading these now to see if they help us make sense of what we have learned so far. [Now read the 'sidebar' or 'caption' text.] You know, I think that adds to what we know. Let's pause for a moment and see what we know just from reading this one spread: (1) bats sleep upside down; (2) bats hang by their toenails; (3) bats have 'beady,' or small eyes; (4) bats have 'pixie,' or small, playful ears; (5) bats have 'thistledown,' or soft fur; (6) bats' wings are made of very fine skin that you can almost see through; (7) bats 'unfurl,' or unfold their wings; (8) there are different kinds of bats and the one we are reading about is called a pipistrelle bat; (9) the pipistrelle bat's body is no bigger than your thumb; (10) a bat's wing is its arm and hand; (11) the skin of the wing is supported by four extra-long fingers. Would you believe there were 11 things for us to learn on those two pages? So when we are reading books to learn about something new it is helpful to read it more than once. And it is helpful to slow down and think about what we are finding out; that helps us to stack it up and make sense of it."

The Conditions of Learning

Consider how we might set the stage to make the read-aloud experience an essential part of our instruction. Brian Cambourne (1988) sets out conditions of learning that I find very helpful when thinking about this. He contends that learning flourishes under these conditions:

- Immersion
- Demonstration
- Engagement
- Expectation
- Responsibility
- Use
- Approximation
- Response

Immersion

Immersion implies that the student is living in the midst of what we value and what we hope they will learn. From my view, though, it does not mean one intense exposure for a period of time, nor does it mean that we litter the physical and emotional environment with examples. To be immersed, in my view, is to live in the midst of something, to have repeated exposure across time, to see numerous functional applications of it.

Immersion in our classrooms can take an example from a candle maker. One way of making candles is to drape a long wick over a dowel rod. The two ends of the wick are lowered into vats of hot wax (they are immersed). The wick isn't left in the wax for very long at a time; rather, it is lifted out, and the dowel is suspended above the vat. As the hot wax drips down the wick, it cools and hardens, forming a mass near the end of the wick. The candle maker understands the need for patience in this process and allows the wax to cool and harden before dipping the developing candle into the wax a second time. On this second dip (immersion), the candle maker, who knows the importance of timing, dips the developing candles into the wax and out again quickly so as not to melt away what has already been accumulated. Once again the dowel is suspended, and the hot wax drips slowly down the emerging candle, forming an even more substantial base. Once again the candle maker waits for the accumulated wax to set. The process is repeated until the accumulated mass is sufficient to meet the intentions of the candle maker.

The key is patient, repeated, well-timed exposure to the hot wax. Consider how the result would have been different if the candle maker approached the process with the belief that extended time in the wax was more important than brief but frequent exposure. The wick would have been draped over the dowel just as in the example above. It would have been lowered into the vat exactly as above. But in this situation the candle maker would have simply left it there, believing that the longer the wick remained in the wax the bigger the candle he would pull up from the wax. Now, if the candle maker had acted on that belief, we know that he would have pulled out a very saturated wick with no greater accumulation of wax than in the first dip of the example above.

Now consider yet another possibility. What if the candle maker had been so pleased by the result of the first dip and cooling cycle in the first example above that he decided to make the second dip twice as long, in hopes of accumulating twice as much mass? Of course, we realize that all the accumulation from the first dip would simply melt away, leaving that poor candle maker frustrated and bewildered.

So in the case of candle making, it is important to have time in the hot wax (that is, to immerse the wick in the wax). But it is also clear that more frequent and well-timed exposure makes for a more substantial candle. The application of this for our classrooms seems simple. Immersion is about repeated exposure over time. Immersion is about having students live in the presence of that which we hope they learn and adopt. Immersion is about having the opportunity to live in the daily functional application of that which is to be learned. However, I am cautious about filling our wall space and every board with charts and print of all sorts in the name of immersion. I am concerned that is more like the candle maker leaving the wick in the hot wax for a few days believing that he'll pull out a beautiful candle. Immersion, in my view, is about exposure over time, at the right time, and for a very clear intention.

Let's think back to reading aloud to inspire. That is immersion. We read to students from very carefully selected texts. We read to them with a clear intention. We don't do it all day long, every day, for months. We read to them at a specific time, and they come to expect it. The exposure is the point. Exposure—immersion in the beauty and rhythm of the language—*is* the purpose. Here the application of knowledge, skill, and strategy, the sound of language, the rhythm of books and poems and feature articles, the captivating trance of a well-told story is not contrived or forced; rather, it is a living part of the classroom community. I would caution us to avoid the temptation to take this to an extreme. Immersion, from my perspective, is repeated exposure in layers and small doses. It is about accumulating learning without even knowing it. It is, as Frank Smith (1998) has said, learning from the company we keep. And in this case, reading to inspire, we are in the company of greatness. We sit huddled together, shoulder to shoulder, knee to knee, in the presence of E. B. White and Patricia MacLachlan, Cynthia Rylant and Katherine Paterson, Tony Johnston and Gary Paulsen, Mem Fox and Jacqueline Woodson, and the list goes on and on. We gather as a community of learners, as a club of language lovers and word-aholics. We gather to soak it up and feast on it until the next time we have an opportunity for the club to meet.

Demonstration

Demonstration, as I see it, is about having a mentor or master perform functional examples in your presence. Cambourne (1988) contends that learning is most efficient when students are immersed in demonstrations of that which we intend for them to learn. If we return to the candle maker, we can see how demonstration might work. Suppose the candle maker works in one of those living history museums where he spends his day making candles the old-fashioned way. All day he is providing demonstrations for others to watch. His work is done in clear view of those who pass through; some are interested in history, or candle making, or the functional crafts of the time. Throughout the day he demonstrates the process of candle making. He also demonstrates the function of each aspect of the process, the patience required, and the importance of the timing involved. And if we were to spend enough time with him, I am most certain we will begin to gain insight, and perhaps even interest in the craft of candle making. We will begin to understand the purpose of lifting the developing candles from the wax and allowing them to drip and cool and harden. We will begin to understand the patience required. We will gain these insights from the "company we keep."

Engagement

To follow Cambourne's conditions for learning, those demonstrations must engage the minds of our students; they must connect and seem worthwhile. Cambourne refers to this as engagement. For this to occur, the demonstrations must be functional and relevant. In our example, the candle maker can't control the engagement of the audience, but he can control some of the conditions that may increase the likelihood of engagement. For example, if the candle maker is passive (just goes about the business of making candles while completely ignoring the audience), there is little to engage the visitors unless they entered with an interest in candle making. If, on the other hand, the candle maker speaks to each group of visitors as they enter, introduces himself, and begins talking about the process of making candles, the likelihood of capturing the interest of those visitors is increased. If he initiates a conversation about how often they use candles and whether they have ever wondered how candles were made and when candles were first used, then the likelihood of an exchange of ideas and conversation is increased even more.

We cannot make learners engage in our demonstrations as teachers, but we can set the stage by seeking connections between what we teach and who our students are as people. When we set the conditions to make learning personal and relevant, we increase the possibility of engagement. I like to think of engagement as something like a radio. Radio stations are broadcasting all the time, but radios are not always picking up the signal. If you switch your radio on, you must *tune in* to a specific station. You can't tune in to all the stations at once. I think of engagement as *tuning in*, intentionally selecting to attend to the demonstration. So ultimately the audience, student, or listener is in control of engagement. Whether we turn to the candle maker, the radio, or a classroom as an example, the learner must make that choice to tune in to the demonstration. And in that sense both the candle maker and the audience have a responsibility. The teacher (candle maker) has a responsibility to make the demonstration relevant and interesting. The audience (the students) has a responsibility to tune in, to attend, or to engage in the demonstration.

Does that mean that when we read aloud we are just filling the fresh air with sound? Oh, I hope not, but yes, it is entirely possible. Think about the candle maker and the opportunity he has to engage his audience as they enter. Think about how the candle maker seeks to make a connection between his demonstrations and the lives and interests of his audience. Can't we follow that example when we read aloud? Do we not know much, much more about our audience than the candle maker knows about his? And will this knowledge of the personalities and interests of our students not serve us well as we prepare our demonstrations? Clearly, then, we can increase the possibility of engagement by careful book selection, offering a bit of introduction to each book before we read it, making connections between the titles, topics, authors, and the interests of our students. We can read with our voice tuned to the tone of the book, the pacing of the language, the shifts in intensity as the text unfolds, and the overall mood of the text. There are ways we can work to bridge those connections and set conditions that may leave our students wanting to hear our next read aloud. Consider that each time we read aloud to inspire and each time we read aloud to invest, we are laying groundwork that increases possibilities of our students' engaging in future instruction. Through consistent demonstrations of artful read alouds, we increase the possibility of having children pause, turn toward our "reading spot," and wait in anticipation as they see us open a book preparing to read.

Think about Frank Smith's notion of learning from the company we keep. He contends that learning is happening all the time as we hang out in the "clubs" we choose to belong to. Engagement, to me, is something like choosing those clubs. Something captures our attention and we tune in as we are deciding whether it is a club we want to be part of. We can tune in just long enough to "learn" whether it is of sufficient interest or use to warrant our time. As we pass through the candle maker's exhibit, for example, some of us would move through without pause. Others may pause to observe and may even comment on how interesting it is to witness. Some may participate in the conversation with the candle maker and inquire about the process. A few may even make return visits with more questions each time. And there will be, of course, those who join the club of candle makers. When we read aloud we have a captive audience—physically, at least. If we wish to captivate their attention, that is, to have them engage in the experience, then we must select books with great care and render an artful delivery of the text. The fact that we hold a book in our hands, fill the air with sound, and demand their physical attention is no guarantee of engagement. Nor is it evidence of such.

Expectation

Expectation in the model outlined by Cambourne is twofold in my mind. One part of that is grounded in clear communication. As the teacher, we must make our expectations for students and our expectations for our demonstrations clear to our learners. The candle maker is going to let you know that he expects you to leave knowing how candles were made in an earlier era. He will direct your attention to the aspect of the process he wants you to notice. As the candle maker lifts the wicks from the vats of hot wax, he isn't likely to say, "Wow, look at that little spider crawling up the wall by the front door." Even if there were a spider by the door he wouldn't divert your attention in that manner. Instead, his expectation is that you will tune in to the process of making candles. Therefore he will keep his attention focused on the process by explaining why he lifts the wicks from the vats and hangs the dowel rod for a while.

To bring this back to our work with read alouds, consider the importance of simply saying why you selected the book, what you hope your students will gain from it, and what you hold as expectations for them when the book is finished. Let's assume for example, that you have selected to read *Bat Loves the Night* by Nicola Davies, with illustrations by Sarah Fox-Davies. Now let's consider what you might say in each of these three situations.

1. Reading aloud to inspire:

"Today we are going to read *Bat Loves the Night* by Nicola Davies, with illustrations by Sarah Fox-Davies. As I read, I hope you'll enjoy the way her writing is almost like a poem. Just listen to the rhythm and the words she chooses. And notice how the art lets us follow a tiny pipistrelle bat through one day."

2. Reading aloud to invest:

"Today we are going to read *Bat Loves the Night* by Nicola Davies, with illustrations by Sarah Fox-Davies. In a few days we will begin a study of bats. As usual, we will begin with sharing our perceptions and charting what we believe to be true about bats. So today as I read, keep that in mind and think about the kind of information you might contribute to the chart next Tuesday. Also, there are two words I want to call to your attention, *echolocation* and *nocturnal.* You may have heard these words before, but today as you listen think about what they mean for the pipistrelle bats. Remember, we'll visit this book again next Tuesday, so just relax and think about bats."

3. Reading aloud to instruct:

"Today we are going to read *Bat Loves the Night* by Nicola Davies, with illustrations by Sarah Fox-Davies. Before we begin, let's revisit the chart we made on Tuesday. Notice how we clustered our thinking about bats. Remember, we listed our ideas about habitats in green and our ideas about their diet and nutrition in blue, and in this section we listed our thoughts about their physical characteristics in red. Then, over here in black, we listed all the myths we have heard about bats. Let's just quickly read through our perceptions and thoughts before we begin the read aloud. [Allow time for that.] Now, as I read today, listen carefully. When you hear something in the text that supports our thinking and proves that it is true, just give me a thumbs-up. I'll stop as soon as I find a good place and we can talk about what you noticed. Also, listen for information that causes you to question some of our thinking. If you hear anything that makes you think our ideas might be incorrect, just let me know with a quiet thumbs-down. Again, I'll stop as soon as I find a good spot, and we will revisit and revise the chart. When we finish, we will see if we might fine-tune our thinking a little bit. Then we can ask better questions, and tomorrow I have another book that has even more information about bats."

It could be that simple. Just make clear what you expect them to do while you read and communicate your intentions for follow-up.

Use

Use in this model is a bit different from practice, as I see it. I often think of practice as something done under orders, a requirement of sorts. I think of use in this model as making practical application of what was witnessed/ learned in the demonstrations... something like attempting to replicate the model. That may be a practice of sorts, but to me practice implies doing something over and over and over for a specified time period each day (basketball drills, playing scales on piano, etc.). Granted, the one who is practicing may love every minute of it. That makes a difference, of course. However, in school, my idea of use is the act of designing opportunities for students to try something out, to explore and attempt the behavior or skill in ways that provide purposeful application that helps children make a connection between the action and its function. So when we read aloud with these conditions of learning in mind, we would follow up with opportunities for students to explore books, share stories, extend the text through art and dance and drama, or launch an inquiry project from their interests. Making clear connections for them to know where they might find books and other texts similar to what we have read aloud will invite them in to the club, so to speak. And that leads them to attempt emulation of the behavior in contexts that make sense for them—*use*.

Approximation

Approximation is an attempt to emulate the demonstration for your own purpose with a product or result that resembles the demonstration. A wonderful example of approximation can be found in the Peter Reynolds story *Ish*. In this simple picture book, a young artist named Ramon is passionate about drawing. He is content and so proud of his work until his brother criticizes it. He vows to do no more drawing. He then discovers that his sister Marisol has made a gallery of his drawings on her bedroom wall. Marisol points to her favorite, and Ramon says it was "supposed to be a vase of flowers... but it doesn't look like one." Marisol saves the day and the artist when she promptly announces, "Well, it looks vase-ISH!"

The "ish" quality is the essence of approximation. It is that stepping toward the ideal we hold in our mind's eye. It is the slow fine-tuning of our own attempts as we work under the influence of the demonstrations we have from the company we keep. We see evidence of approximation when we hear students reading aloud to peers or presenting their work with attention to the qualities of an artful read aloud. We see the influence of our demonstrations each time we see them attempting to grow toward the ways we make books and reading and writing a central part of all our work together. We see them fine-tuning their own work as they seek out books and other text to accompany the projects they undertake. Approximation is a natural consequence of attempting something new—even for adults. We would be wise to remember that an approximation is clear evidence that students engaged in our demonstration and found it worthy enough to attempt it for themselves. It isn't always about the product, the result, or the score.

Response

The final condition in Cambourne's model is response. It is clear that response is a form of feedback. How we respond can encourage further approximations and more engagement in more demonstrations—or shut the student down completely. Simply revisit the example above in the Peter Reynolds book. Ramon's brother offered criticism: "Leon burst out laughing, 'WHAT is THAT?' he asked." Criticism, in my view, is offered to harm; it is negative feedback that isn't intended to help the recipient grow. It is meant to cut, to demean, to make the critic feel more powerful, perhaps. Critique, on the other hand, is offered to help the recipient to note what worked well and where the work may need a bit of fine-tuning. In *Ish*, Marisol offers critique when she doesn't give Ramon false praise saying his drawing is the most beautiful, realistic rendition of a vase of flowers. Instead, she points to the qualities that are its strength and compliments him when she says, "Well, it looks vase-ISH!" That bit of response from a caring other, from one whose opinion is valued and trusted, moves the student forward toward fine-tuning the results. Marisol's response reignited Ramon's faith in himself and set him on a new course. In much the same way, our responses to any student attempts will be among our most powerful interactions with them. So when we read aloud, keep in mind that their approximations are the most flattering of actions. They are emulating a behavior they deem most worthy. They are emulating the actions of one they hold in high esteem. How we respond has tremendous power. Our very responses can shape their respect for us, their interest in reading and writing and literature, and even have great power over how they view themselves as worthy and smart.

Making Read Aloud Intentional: One Possibility

Let's take the time to look closely at the role of read aloud in a subject matter unit of study. Assume for this example that you are planning a study of bats in your science curriculum. You might begin by gathering the students on the carpet with a whiteboard or large chart nearby. And it would go something like this:

> "Each of you has heard of bats, right? But do you know much about them? Let's just take a minute to think about bats. Close your eyes if that helps you think, but focus on bats. I want you to search your mind and try to find all the bits of information you have tucked away in there. Hold on, I just need you to think right now about what a bat looks like. So get focused and try to picture a bat in your mind. Take a close look and try to remember all the details you can. Got it? Let's think for a moment."

Pause here for about 45 seconds.

> "Now turn to the person next to you and talk for 40 seconds about what you saw in your mind."

I actually time this.

> "Tell all the details you can and remember to listen to your partner as well.

> "Eyes up here, please. Talkers off. Thinkers on. Now, tell me something you heard someone else say that you think we should put on our list."

As children respond, I record what they say in blue and cluster it all together. Note that you will likely find some responses that are factual and some that are not. List them all and make it clear that you will list anything that is believed to be true. The purpose of this list is to generate a baseline of our thinking.

"Wow, we have quite a list here."

The list may include things such as *bats are black*, *bats have wings*, *they have small ears*, *their skin is like leather*, *bats have tiny beady eyes*, *they have fangs*, and so on.

> "Now I need you to think again. Talkers off. Thinkers on. Ready? This time I want to you think, no talking yet, just think about where bats live. Try to picture all the places you might find bats if you went on a bat hunt. Where are those places? What does it look like there? Do the bats have houses, or nests, or crawl into tiny holes, or something else? Think about that for a few more seconds. When we open our eyes, I'll ask you to turn and share your thinking with the person next to you. Remember to listen and share because I'll ask you to tell me something your partner said to you. Ready? Talk with your partner for forty seconds."

This time, when you draw their focus back to you, move to a different section of the chart and write in a different color, green for example. This way you create clusters of information that can be grouped under headings they are likely to find in an index.

> "Let's get your thinking listed here. I'm writing in green this time and I'll put your ideas in this corner. That way we can keep our ideas about what bats look like and our ideas about where bats live separate."

When the list is complete, you will likely have ideas such as *bats live in caves*, *they live in dark places*, *they live under bridges*, *they live in trees*, *they live in the attic*, etc. Again, remember that you are getting a baseline of their perceptions. This is not about getting factual information.

> "Let's get focused again. Talkers off. Thinkers on. This time, I need you to think about what bats eat. I want you to close your eyes and think about a bat going to dinner. Where does the bat go? Do all the bats go together, or do they each go alone? What sort of food do they eat? Do they search for food? Where do they find it? Does the bat collect the food and bring it back to share? Or does the bat eat the food right where it is found? OK, just think for a bit."

While they are thinking, I am getting a red marker so I can continue to cluster information by heading and color to help them organize their thoughts and develop understandings during the upcoming read aloud.

> "Eyes open. Turn to your partner and share your thoughts. Remember to be a good listener as well so you can report something interesting you heard. Ready? You have forty seconds. Remember, you need to share your thinking and listen to the thinking of your partner."

I continue to stress the need to listen at this time, as most children are eager to share their own ideas. I am trying to lead them toward understanding that they can learn from listening to others. As they share their thoughts, I record them in another section of the chart using the red marker.

I continue with this, keeping the focus on habitat, mating, and reproduction, diet and nutrition, physical characteristics, and movement from place to place, but I like to end this one with myths and misunderstandings about bats. So let's skip down to that.

> "Take a look at our thinking. Wow, you all have filled two chart sheets with your thoughts about bats! Well, I have one more thing I want you to think about before we begin to investigate. Blink twice if you are ready to think. Remember, talkers off, thinkers on. This time I want to think about all the myths and misunderstandings people tell about bats. Think for a minute about all the things you have ever heard about bats. Think about some of the things you have heard people say because they are afraid of bats. Think about some of the things you have heard people say because they have never even seen a bat. Just think about that. What are the things you've heard that you think are not really true?"

Pause for a moment to let them think while you get the black marker ready.

> "Eyes open. Turn to your partner. Remember you have forty seconds to share your thoughts and also listen to your partner's ideas."

Remember to keep this tightly focused and quick. I try to stay within the 40 seconds so they will get to the point and stay energized about the topic. It seems to lend a sense of urgency to the whole brainstorming session.

"So let's get your thinking listed on our chart. Ready? Let me hear some of the things you heard from your partner."

I continue with listing out what they say, this time in black so each cluster of ideas is in a separate section and in a different color.

"We have one more task before we begin the read aloud and start our investigation into the life of bats. Let's take a look at our chart. Each section is in a different color, and each section is our thinking around one idea about bats. Let's look at the green section, where we were thinking about where bats live. Can you think of a word we might find in our science book or in other nonfiction books that means where an animal lives?"

Students will generate a list of words like *homes*, *houses*, *shelter*. If they do not get there, I will introduce the word *habitat*.

"So let's make a heading for the green section on this chart and call it Habitat."

Repeat this for each section on the chart, using headings that are likely to be found in the index, table of contents, or glossary of resources you plan to use.

"Now we have our thinking up here and ready for our study. Tomorrow we will begin with a read aloud called *Bat Loves the Night* by Nicola Davies, with illustrations by Sarah Fox-Davies."

The next day, gather your students so they can see the charts and the details in the text and the art of the book you will feature.

"Yesterday we spent a lot of time just getting our thinking about bats organized on these charts. Take a look; we have thoughts on habitats and physical characteristics, diet and nutrition, mating and reproduction, movement, habits, myths and misunderstandings, and more. We did a lot of thinking didn't we? Let's quickly read through our perceptions and thoughts before we begin the read aloud."

Allow time for this quick review.

"Today we are going to read *Bat Loves the Night* by Nicola Davies, with illustrations by Sarah Fox-Davies. You may remember that we read this book last week and I told you then we would be studying bats. Remember, I asked you to notice two words—*nocturnal* and *echolocation*? As I read the book again today, I would like you to listen carefully and think about what we listed on our charts. When you hear something in the text that supports our thinking and proves that it is true, just give me a quiet thumbs-up. I'll stop as soon as I find a good place, and we can talk about what you noticed. Also listen for information that causes you to question some of our thinking. If you hear anything that makes you think our ideas might be incorrect, just let me know with a quiet thumbs-down. Again, I'll stop as soon as I find a good spot, and we will revisit and revise the chart. When we finish, we will see if we are able to fine-tune our thinking on the charts. Then we can ask better questions, and tomorrow I'll have another book that has even more information about bats."

This second reading of a picture book gives them some familiar territory as we begin reading aloud to instruct—to stretch their thinking and have them revise some of their misunderstanding and misperceptions. As you read along, there will be several places where you can pause to verify and validate the thinking they have listed on the chart. Take the time to signify that validation. I like to simply place a small plus sign to the left of the item on the list. When there is conflict between the information we are gaining from a read aloud and the ideas we have on the chart, I prefer to signal that with a question mark. The reason for this is it calls our attention to the need for us to check our thinking as we delve into the read alouds that will follow this one.

"Let's take a look at the way our thinking was stretched by this book."

Review the chart, drawing attention to the validations and revisions.

"Now that we know more about bats, I'm thinking we could ask some good questions to focus our investigation. Let's go back to our categories here on the chart. Shall we begin with Habitat? We found out that bats do prefer dark places like the attic of a house or a cave. Does that leave you with any questions?"

List the questions that arise from revisiting the thinking that was validated or revised and continue a similar process with each of the sections.

"Tomorrow we will read another book about bats. It is called *Bats* by Gail Gibbons. It is more of an all-about information book. When we read it, I am sure we will find answers to some of our questions from today. I think we will also find some new information to add to our charts."

I will continue this for two or three days, each day reading a book that is more complex, more detailed, more specific than the one before. This process allows each book to scaffold for the ones to follow and enables the students to accumulate information in layers. Each layer of information creates a base for the next, giving the students enough background to make sense of the next layer.

Once again, here are a few books you might find useful in this particular example:

- *Bat Loves the Night* by Nicola Davies

- *Bats* by Gail Gibbons

- *Bats* by Nancy J. Shaw

- *Bats* by Margaret Dornfeld

As you read each book, you will have opportunities to model the use of an index to look for specific information, to address a question, or to return to a page to find a detail to resolve some confusion or disagreement, such as when two students remember the detail differently. You will also be able to immerse your students in demonstrations of the use of a table of contents, the glossary, headings in text, and bold print in a nonfiction book as opposed to bold print in a fiction book. Many opportunities will present themselves.

Reading Aloud
Often and Well:
The Art of Read Aloud

For just a few moments, try to conjure up an image in your mind of a parent holding a toddler and telling a story. Perhaps the story is "Goldilocks and the Three Bears" or "The Gingerbread Man" or "Little Red Riding Hood." It might even be a simple nursery rhyme such as "Little Miss Muffet." Now that you have the image, lean in and listen to the telling of the story. Listen to the voice of the storyteller and notice the differences in the pitch when Papa Bear speaks and when Mama Bear speaks. Notice how the pacing changes as the tension in the story begins to mount. Listen to the storyteller stretch out words like "great big papa bear bowl" and increase the speed to push words together when the action is fast-paced. Notice as you listen to the shift in the voice when a character is frightened or angry or excited. When we tell stories, it seems almost natural for us to unconsciously attend to the significant role that tone, intensity, pacing, and mood can play in helping the child make sense of the story. It seems natural as a scaffold for comprehension when we are telling our little ones a story. Before you let go of that image, take a look at the face of the storyteller. You probably notice facial expressions and body language and hand gestures that attempt to make the language easier to understand. Each aspect of the storyteller's rendition of the story is a layer to help the child make meaning, to engage the child in the story, and to create a bond between the humans involved.

> "There's no exact right way of reading aloud, other than to try to be as expressive as possible. As we read a story, we need to be aware of our body posture, our eyes and their expression, our eye contact with the child or children, our vocal variety, and our general facial animation. But each of us will have our own special way of doing it."
>
> —Mem Fox (2001, p. 40)

Indulge me further and conjure a second image. This time, picture an adult reading a book aloud to a small group of children. The group may be siblings, cousins, or friends gathered for a party, a sleepover, or a playdate. The group may be a group of schoolchildren. Let's say the book is a picture book. Now lean in and listen. Do you hear those shifts in pitch to signal a different character is speaking? Do you hear the elongations of selected words being stretched for emphasis? Do you hear the pacing change when the action is mounting? Do you see the reader using facial expressions or hand gestures that match the story? For some reason, these things seem less natural to adults in a read aloud than in storytelling.

Reading aloud well borrows from the art of storytelling. To present the text with an accurate rendition of the words without attention to tone and intensity and mood and pacing is like leaving the icing off the cake. To read aloud without attention to rhythm, pitch, and stress makes the sound of the reading expressionless, less robust, less meaningful, just . . . less. To read aloud well, the reader, like the storyteller, must attend to at least these four qualities.

1. **Tone** I think of the tone of the text as the feel of the piece. Is it light, informal, deep, dark, or formal? Like the hues of a color, is it rich and robust, or soft and subtle? The writer's attitude and feeling toward the subject will set the tone. Tone may also reflect what the writer intends to make the reader feel. This interpretation will be reflected in the voice quality of the reader.

2. **Mood** I think of the mood of a text as the emotional climate of the piece, its temperament or attitude. Is it sad, depressed, hopeful, wishful, excited, eager, or nostalgic? As we reach the end of the reading, the mood should linger like a fine fragrance.

3. **Intensity** I think of intensity as the energy of the text. Is it powerful and bold, or tender and quiet? Does the energy build and wane? Or does it launch with a punch and remain at that level? Or does it begin full and slowly dwindle? Perhaps it is quiet and gentle from the first line to the last. The intensity of a piece will be reflected in a read aloud by the shifts in volume and the power of the reader's voice.

4. **Pacing** I think of pacing as the heartbeat of the text. It is a pulse, a rhythm that creates the flow of the language. It may race at times and slow to heart-stopping standstill

at others. We feel the effect of pacing when the reader's voice employs a dramatic pause or begins rushing to build tension. We feel the effect when a reader's voice moves as slow as honey on a February morning to draw the listener in. It may be heard and felt when a reader stretches a word for emphasis or runs through words like a babbling brook to reflect the action of the piece.

Reading aloud well is like playing music. As the reader, you are a musician of sorts and your instrument is your voice. Not only must you (the reader) be able to "read" the words with accuracy, you must also be able to interpret the intentions of the writer regarding tone, intensity, pacing, and mood. The texts we read aloud for our students have signals that indicate the intentions of writers (and the team of people who work in layout and design to produce a book) that are in many ways like the signals provided by composers for musicians.

"The ups and downs of our voices and our pauses and points of emphasis are like music, literally, to the ears of young children, and kids love music."

— Mem Fox (2001, p. 40)

For example, in music, when a composer intends for the musician to increase or decrease the intensity of the music, this may be signaled by special marks which look something like an elongated greater-than sign < (increase or *crescendo*) or an elongated less-than sign > (decrease or *decrescendo*). The musician interprets these notations and adjusts the sound or level of intensity when playing. These shifts in intensity not only capture the attention of the listeners but they also help convey the emotional content of the music.

Composers also indicate their intentions regarding the pacing of a piece with a time signature (3/4, 4/4, etc.) indicating the number of beats in each measure. This sets a pace, creates a rhythm for the piece. So a series of whole notes, where each measure is a single note being played for four beats, may seem slow and languid to the ear. However, the composer may create a sense of movement by placing two half-notes, getting two beats each in one measure, followed by measure with four quarter-notes, getting one beat each. And to create a greater sense of urgency, we may find a measure with eighth notes and sixteenth notes. If the composer decides that a span of silence would create a desired effect, that will be signaled by a rest. The use of silence is an important part of music. Silence in well-chosen places draws your attention to the music. The composer can create a feeling or tone with the combination of pacing and intensity.

Readers can find signals regarding intensity and pacing in print as well. Just as composers use visual cues to signal their intentions, writers use punctuation and shifts in font, bold print, underlining and italics, size of print, syllable length, word length and sentence length, line breaks, white space, and more to indicate their intentions regarding intensity in the performance of the text. As a reader, you recognize that a word printed in bold type suggests that you should increase the intensity of your voice. Likewise, when the print becomes gradually smaller, you would let your voice become gradually softer. Intensity may also be signaled with punctuation marks. Every first-grade student clearly understands that an exclamation point signals excitement. Even first graders know that means your voice becomes stronger and louder. If the writer includes more than one exclamation point, all capital letters, bold print, red lettering, and a larger font, you recognize immediately that you are expected to boost the volume and convey some big message. And if you just read right past that, children will stop you in midsentence and point to the writer's signals, letting you know you didn't read that right. As readers, we come to recognize that a question mark at the end of a line signals a shift in intensity and tone, and ellipses indicate that we should either hold the sound and stretch it a bit or let our voices trail off as if there was more to say but it was better left unsaid, or to indicate that there was a word left out deliberately. It is our voice that communicates these purposes to the listener.

> **"From my own experience I realize that the literature I *heard*, rather than read, as a child resonates again and again in my memory whenever I sit down to write."**
>
> — Mem Fox (1993, p. 68)

READ-ALOUD TUTORIAL 2

All the Places to Love
by Patricia MacLachlan

Let's consider how signals in the text might impact our delivery of the music in language when we read aloud. To do this, let's contrast the opening lines of two picture books, *All the Places to Love* and *The Recess Queen*.

All the Places to Love, with art by Mike Wimmer, begins with one sentence placed on the page in three phrases:

On the day I was born

My grandmother wrapped me in a blanket

made from the wool of her sheep.

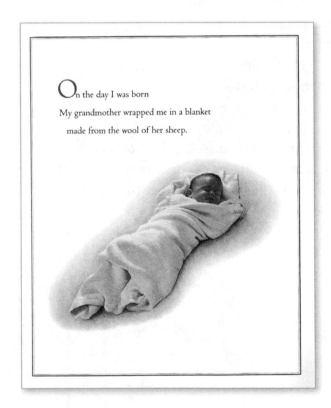

The second page presents the language so that each line begins with a capital letter (as in some poetry), and the line breaks on the right indicate a slow, deliberate pace and a natural place to pause in the sound of language. Note also that these six lines are actually two sentences, and the second sentence ends with a list of three items, indicating a pause after each item in the list:

She held me up in the open window

So that what I heard first was the wind.

What I saw first were all the places to love:

The valley,

The river falling down over rocks,

The hilltop where the blueberries grew.

 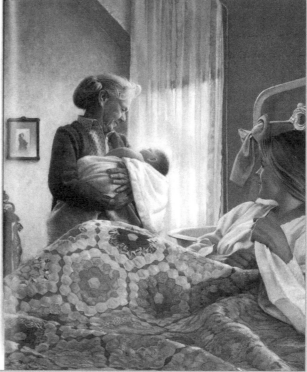

The placement of words, the line breaks, and the use of white space signal a slow, deliberate pace. As I see it, the pacing is established by phrasing that is set up in the line breaks. A slight pause is suggested at the end of each line, just as in the lines of poetry. To get a feel for the difference in the sound of it, try reading the above lines as if they were in a paragraph:

"On the day I was born [m]y grandmother wrapped me in a blanket made from the wool of her sheep. She held me up in the open window [s]o that what I heard first was the wind. What I saw first were all the places to love: [t]he valley, [t]he river falling down over rocks, [t]he hilltop where the blueberries grew."

To read this beautiful, fluid language in a rush is to rob the listener of its music. Reading it in a paragraph without the line breaks, without the pauses, creates a sense of moving through at a steady pace without a pause until you reach an end punctuation mark. It would be somewhat like playing music too fast: You lose something beautiful, something pleasing to the ear. Presenting the language in phrases, with the line breaks in place, suggests the pauses that create that small silence between thoughts. Those little silent spaces offer the brain an opportunity to process each bit of information, layering it into a unified message.

Consider this:

"On the day I was born	[Slight pause.]
My grandmother wrapped me in a blanket	[Slight pause.]
made from the wool of her sheep."	[Full stop.]
"She held me up in the open window	[Slight pause.]
So that what I heard first was the wind.	[Full stop.]
What I saw first were all the places to love:	[Long pause.]
The valley,	[Slight pause.]
The river falling down over rocks,	[Slight pause.]
The hilltop where the blueberries grew."	[Full stop.]

Now try reading it aloud. Listen to your own voice and try to shift the pacing as indicated above. Try it two or three times until you find a rhythm that sounds natural and sounds as if you are presenting something of value in each line. Contrast that with a reading of the paragraph format presented at top.

What you notice is the music in the language. It's a rhythm that will tease the ear and engage the mind of listeners when you read aloud and attend to the *sound print* of the writer's voice. We talk about style and voice when we teach our students to write. In writer's workshop and when conferring, we help children find their own voice by studying the voices of other writers. That is part of using picture books as mentor texts and part of the work we do in the study of craft. Through artful read aloud, we can help children learn to arrest the rhythm of language with their ears, but that will only happen if we are playing the music of that language on the instrument of our voice (to take that music analogy a bit further).

When I read a picture book, I also notice the art, as it helps me interpret the tone of the book. The first page of *All the Places to Love* is a tender image in gentle tones depicting a newborn baby wrapped in a soft, cream-colored blanket (see page 62). The image is realistic, almost like a portrait or a photograph. This tender image immediately suggests a soft tone. It is as if the writer and the illustrator are signaling the reader to speak quietly (to let this little baby sleep) in much the same way a composer would signal the musician with *p (piano),* indicating the intention to play softly, quietly.

So in the opening pages of most any book there are signals to suggest how the reader might deliver the text. We see signals in the line breaks and punctuation, in the spacing and placement of phrases. We also see signals in the palate of color, in the style of the art and images themselves. As readers who will deliver the text to listeners, we can make the whole event more robust, more memorable if we attend to those signals.

All the Places to Love

by Patricia MacLachlan

Tone
The overall tone of this read aloud is gentle and caring.

Intensity
Energy in this book is steady and flowing. It is smooth and silky.

Pacing
The pace matches the energy and is a gentle flowing stream of beautiful language. This book should not be rushed.

Mood
The general mood of this book is peaceful, graceful, kind, and loving.

Read-Aloud Tutorial

When Preparing for a Read-Aloud Experience Consider

- Consider the artwork—do the colors suggest a bold, boisterous voice or a quiet, more subdued tone; is there movement and energy calling for a more rapid pace and greater intensity, or is the art more static and peaceful, calling for a slower, softer voice?

- Read the dedication yourself and share it with your students if there is additional insight offered there—the dedication can offer a window into the author's motives and connections to the text.

- Examine the endpapers—these often carry a motif or design from the text, giving insight into a theme or feeling for the book that can influence your presentation of the language.

- Consider the genre and what you know and expect from texts written in that genre—a biography would be read with different emphasis than humor or poetry, for example.

- Review the author and illustrator information on the flap—this information can provide insight into the influences in the writing or illustration style, topic, and presentation.

- Preview the book by reading it aloud to yourself ahead of time; listen for the rhythm and find the flow.

- Read the book at least once silently and then once aloud to find the rhythm and note the points in the text where you might need to pause or quicken the pace, drop your voice to a whisper, or build to a near shout.

- Note those places in the text where you may need to pause for a brief comment or scaffold meaning for the audience—avoid overdoing this, and be careful to recognize that it isn't necessary in every book.

- Change the tone of your voice to match the dialogue or the personality of the characters, or to set the mood when possible.

- Adjust your pace to fit the story, slowing down for dramatic pauses and speeding up to create movement and energy.

- Make your voice expressive; convey the emotional quality of the text.

- Know why you are presenting a particular text; be clear about your expectations of the book, your presentation, and the students—let this information guide your voice as it conveys tone and mood through pacing and intensity.

- Position yourself so that both you and the children are comfortable, your voice can carry to the entire group, and the illustrations (if there are any) can be seen.

- Vary the length and subject matter of the read-aloud experience. Include picture books, storybooks, chapter books, nonfiction, and poetry.

- Allow your listeners a few minutes to settle down and adjust their bodies and minds to the story.

- Allow time for (but don't require) discussion after reading.

- Add a third dimension to the book when it will add depth and enhance the experience—for example, bring a bowl of blueberries to be eaten after reading Robert McCloskey's *Blueberries for Sal*.

The Recess Queen by Alexis O'Neill

Let's contrast the signals in a quiet, tender story like *All the Places to Love* with the story of a playground bully. In *The Recess Queen* by Alexis O'Neill, with art by Laura Huliska-Beith, we meet a young girl who is a playground bully. The opening lines on the first spread present the bully:

> **MEAN JEAN was Recess Queen**
>
> **and nobody said any different.**

This first sentence is presented on two lines, again suggesting an emphasis. The first line establishes her identity. The second line makes it clear that identity is unchallenged.

The next page (opposing page on the same spread) presents three sentences that are listed as three separate statements rather than written in paragraph form:

Nobody swung until Mean Jean swung.

Nobody kicked until Mean Jean kicked.

Nobody bounced until Mean Jean bounced.

The language is presented in phrases, just as in *All the Places to Love*. Does that suggest a slow, deliberate pace? Not to me. Note that the first two words in the first sentence are in a different font, all capital letters and in bold print— "**MEAN JEAN**...." That suggests a strong voice, a bold beginning, as if the composer is signaling the musician to begin with *ff* (*fortissimo* or very loud). We open with intensity that helps establish the identity of the main character and sets the tone of dominance a bully works so hard to create. As we continue, the language is presented in a bold, clear, tight font that is unembellished, suggesting to me that we are to keep that tone present as we read.

Let's examine how the presentation of the language actually makes a difference in how we make it sound when we read aloud. By way of contrast, try reading this opening written in paragraph form with a more traditional font, no bold print, and without the use of capital letters at the beginning of the sentence. It would look like this:

Mean Jean was Recess Queen and nobody said any different.
Nobody swung until Mean Jean swung. Nobody kicked until
Mean Jean kicked. Nobody bounced until Mean Jean bounced.

So just read it aloud a few times as if you are reading a paragraph. Of course, if you have read the book aloud many times, you may be influenced by your attention to the features of the print and the presentation of the art. So try to divorce your mind from those influences. Just read the sentences in the paragraph as if you were the anchor on the six o'clock news.... It sounds flat, doesn't it? And you certainly don't leave with a highly emotional response to Jean.

Now let's layer the format back into the presentation. I'll replace the bold and change the font to simulate the presentation in the book:

MEAN JEAN was Recess Queen

and nobody said any different.

Nobody swung until Mean Jean swung.

Nobody kicked until Mean Jean kicked.

Nobody bounced until Mean Jean bounced.

Wow, what a difference that makes! Clearly, this will not sound like the anchor on the six o'clock news. Nor will it have the quiet, tender tone of *All the Places to Love*. This bold print, the enlarged font, and the line breaks suggest something more for me. Consider the following suggestions. Note how the bold print, the selection of font, and the subject (bullying) lead you toward a sense of defiance, a strong voice, a louder voice:

"MEAN JEAN was Recess Queen   [Bold voice to establish her role.]

and nobody said any different."   [Defiant tone, dare anyone to challenge.]

On the next page (opposing page of the same spread), note how the sentences are presented in a list, making the parallel structure quite visible. This creates a listing effect, as if you are making the rules quite clear. It is also introducing the main character and establishing her role as playground bully. That personality is more evident in this presentation:

"Nobody swung until Mean Jean swung.   [Bold, defiant voice; full stop.]

Nobody kicked until Mean Jean kicked.   [Bold, defiant voice; full stop.]

Nobody bounced until Mean Jean bounced."   [Bold, defiant voice; full stop.]

When I consider the art, I have even more signals for interpreting the sound of this book. The illustrations are rendered in bold and bright acrylic and collage, giving the book a strong and vivid look. The opening spread makes a clear statement, with Mean Jean consuming practically all of the first page. Her arms are crossed, her body is leaning in toward the center of the page, and her head is the largest feature on the spread. Her face has a snarky, satisfied grimace and her eyes glare across the spread into a crowd of children clustered somewhat like bowling pins. The faces of the children are wide-eyed, with mouths drawn in tight little O's as they await the signal from Mean Jean letting them know they have her permission to play. The bold color, paired with a perspective that presents a sharp contrast between the size of Jean and the other children, creates a defiant, bold, bullying tone that is supported by the features in the print. These features could create an aggressive feel, but are abated somewhat by the animated style of illustration.

The Recess Queen
by Alexis O'Neill

Tone
The overall tone of this read aloud is bright, quick, a bit aggressive, with a shift at the end toward friendship.

Intensity
Energy runs high in this read aloud. Your voice will need to reflect the high energy of a playground and translate the emotions at play.

Pacing
The pace matches the energy and the quick pulse of moving across a crowded playground.

Mood
The general mood of this book is humor, yet the subject is more serious.

Diary of a Worm by Doreen Cronin

Now let's consider a book that is clearly intended as humor, Doreen Cronin's *Diary of a Worm*, with illustrations by Harry Bliss. Just take a look at the cover. There's a worm with a ball cap on his head, holding a pencil with his tail, "sitting" on a bottle cap, using a mushroom as his desk, while writing intently in an open notebook. Who could take this seriously? I know immediately I am to have fun with this one. The title, in large orange print, is presented in all capitals. That captures my attention. The endpapers of this book present a scrapbook of our cover character and his friends, family, and mementoes. Open the book to any spread and you will see a diary format. There is a date printed in the upper left corner of the page with a narrative capturing an event of that day. Of course, being a diary written by a worm, it is told from a worm's point of view. Therefore, the entire book is filled with "worm humor." All this just layers in the humor and suggests a lighthearted tone that should be reflected in your voice.

Turn to the spread for May 28. Notice that the print is presented with a good bit of space between each idea. There is a small illustration under each cluster of print (four illustrations in all; two on the left page and two on the right). In each of the illustrations we see the "head and shoulders" of six worms in various leaning positions. The text reads:

> MAY 28
>
> Last night I went to the school dance.
> > You put your head in.
> [Illustration shows six worms from the "waist" up, all leaning in.]
>
> > You put your head out.
> [Illustration shows six worms, all leaning out.]
>
> You do the hokey pokey and
> > you turn yourself about.
> [Illustration shows six worms rotating.]
>
> > That's all we could do.
> [Illustration shows six worms standing straight with solemn faces.]

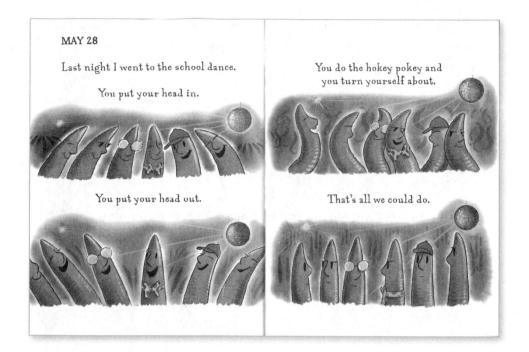

MAY 28

Last night I went to the school dance.

You put your head in.

You put your head out.

You do the hokey pokey and
you turn yourself about.

That's all we could do.

One quick read and you know this is a childhood song with actions. A quick glance at the four illustrations and you recognize the worms are doing the hokey pokey. Recognizing this childhood favorite calls for you to sing the second, third, fourth, and fifth lines.

Try this. Read the brief text as if you are that news anchor again. I'll collapse the text for you to see it as a paragraph:

> "May 28 Last night I went to the school dance. You put your head in. You put your head out. You do the hokey pokey and you turn yourself about. That's all we could do."

To read this as if it were the news renders something that sounds like a bad farce, a *Saturday Night Live* skit gone bad. If we read it with our attention given to accuracy (getting all the words right) and rate (reading it quickly) and don't attend to the music of the language, we get something that sounds less like language and more like nonsense. The humor is lost. The meaning diminishes and the whole effect is deflated.

To sound the music of language, we have to pay attention to other signals in the print, in the layout, in the art, and in the language itself. We have to interpret as we read, make sense of the situation, and let our use of pacing, tone, intensity, and mood reflect those decisions. Looking at the book pages at top, let's examine those signals.

The art is whimsical, almost comic. The expressions and movement of the worms suggest frivolity in the first three scenes and a deadpan solemnity in the final scene.

The language blends a narrative and lyrics from a song. The spacing suggests four quick and successive scenes recording one event.

This time, try reading it as if you were telling a friend about the evening:

MAY 28

"Last night I went to the school dance.   [Read like you are telling a friend what you did last night. If you went to a dance you probably were excited. Let your voice show that.]

You put your head in.   [Sing the first line of the familiar song. Slight pause.]

You put your head out.   [Sing the second line. Slight pause.]

You do the hokey pokey and   [Sing the third and fourth lines. Full stop. Let there be some silence before the next line.]

you turn yourself about.

That's all we could do."   [Stand still. Drop all expression from your face and deliver this last line in a very solemn tone.]

Next, let's take a look at the April 10 entry to see how pacing can further influence the power of the read aloud:

APRIL 10

It rained all night and the ground

was soaked. We spent the entire day

on the sidewalk.

Hopscotch is a very dangerous game.

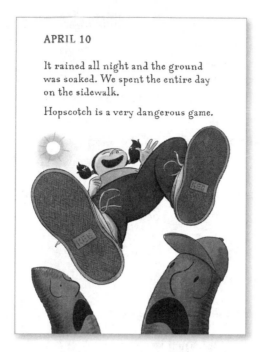

APRIL 10

It rained all night and the ground
was soaked. We spent the entire day
on the sidewalk.

Hopscotch is a very dangerous game.

When looking at a read aloud, I take signals for pacing from the use of white space, line breaks, and the rhythm in the language itself. In this example, I can't rely on the line breaks for a sense of pacing because they are determined by the size of the page. In other words, each line runs to the end of the page and returns when the margin is reached. So there does not appear to be any deliberate attempt to influence the pace with an intentional line break.

So next, I look to the language for cues. These three sentences are presenting four ideas:

1. It rained all night.

2. The ground was soaked.

3. We spent all day on the sidewalk.

4. Hopscotch is a dangerous game.

So to make sure the listeners get all four ideas as I read, I will pause slightly after each idea. I do that in an effort to help my audience build and layer an understanding. As you look back to the text you will see that the first section ends with the word *sidewalk*. Then there is an extra line space before the next sentence, as if adding another paragraph. Note the four ideas presented. The first three are connected to explain why the worm family spent a day on the sidewalk. It is something like the setup in a joke. The fourth idea, that hopscotch is dangerous, is only funny if you think about it from the worm's perspective.

A long pause between the third idea and the fourth allows the audience to create a scene, see the rain soaking into the ground, flooding little worm homes, and to imagine the worms moving up and out to safety. That image has to settle before you drop the idea about hopscotch, or the two will not connect.

Try this out. I'll present the exact language, but I'll reformat it so that it appears as one block of text.

> **APRIL 10**
>
> **It rained all night and the ground**
>
> **was soaked. We spent the entire day**
>
> **on the sidewalk. Hopscotch is a very**
>
> **dangerous game.**

Now read it as if you were reading a paragraph. Read with no pauses beyond what you would normally layer in for a period. Read it aloud two or three times, trying to keep the pace even. Do you notice how the last idea seems out of place without that long pause?

Try one more thing. Let's attend to tone and intensity this time. The overall tone is light and fun. The intensity (energy, pitch, passion) is moderate. There is a shift in tone between the third idea and the fourth one. The tone of the first three ideas (the first two sentences) is somewhat neutral reporting of fact, so the intensity would be lessened here. If it were music, we might see *mf (mezzo forte)* written in beneath the music.

APRIL 10

It rained all night and the ground

was soaked. We spent the entire day

on the sidewalk.

Hopscotch is a very dangerous game.

But that line space signals a rest, a full-measure rest. So after reading the first two sentences in a neutral tone (not anxious, not eager, not worried), allow a long pause. That bit of silence builds tension, layers suspense, and, most importantly, allows the audience to process the three ideas in those first two sentences. Now drop the last idea, the third sentence, on them. *Drop* is the appropriate term here. I actually drop my voice, lower my tone, stepping out of that neutral tone and into a more somber, more worried tone of voice to read the final sentence. That shift creates a contrast that spikes the humor in the passage.

Diary of a Worm
by Doreen Cronin

Tone
The overall tone of this read aloud is light, easy, and fun.

Intensity
Energy shifts very little throughout the reading of this text. There are places where you drop your voice to show a shift in the emotional tone.

Pacing
Overall, the pace of this read aloud is rather steady. There are places where pauses are necessary to deliver the "punchline." In those places, silence is actually helpful, as it draws attention to the shift.

Mood
The general mood of this book is upbeat, light-hearted, and humorous with a positive feeling.

READ-ALOUD TUTORIAL 4

Snow Day! by Lester Laminack

Intensity in the read aloud can be examined with *Snow Day!* by Lester Laminack. This book (yes, I wrote it) is a story of anticipation—living through those hours between the weatherman's prediction for significant snowfall and the morning after. The intensity or energy in this book is evident from the first line and continues at a high level to the last line. Let's step inside:

> Did you *hear* that?
>
> Did the weatherman just say what I
>
> thought he did?
>
> Did he say...
>
> **SNOW?**
>
> Oh please, let it snow. Lots and lots of snow.

First notice the short sentences dancing back and forth on the page. Notice the word *snow* popping out at you. This is *the* announcement that snow is on the way. That builds energy and anticipation in most households with school-

age children (or at least one teacher). That energy calls for intensity in your voice when you read aloud.

Imagine reading this aloud to your students as if you were that six o'clock news anchor:

> "Did you hear that? Did that weatherman just say what I thought he did? Did he say... SNOW? Oh please, let it snow. Lots and lots of snow."

Even this presentation of the print zaps energy from this much-anticipated event. Consider it again in the original form:

"Did you *hear* that? [The narrator is speaking directly to you. Notice the italics used for emphasis, nudging you to punch up the intensity there.]

Did the weatherman just say what I thought he did? [Notice the space between the first line and this one, signaling you to pause. It's as if you are waiting to hear from the weatherman again. Your voice calls to the listener to confirm what you heard, engaging the audience.]

Did he say... [Notice the hesitation, the trailing off marked by the ellipses.]

SNOW? [How could you miss this cue? Notice the enlarged font, the use of all capitals, and bold print begging you to significantly increase the intensity.]

Oh please, let it snow. Lots and lots of snow." [This is a plea. Let your voice plead with the audience.]

In this presentation, the placement of text, the use of font size and italics and bold, the series of three questions, and a plea all work together to build the energy of a possible snowfall and the hope for a snow day. So when you read it aloud, the intensity of your voice should reflect that energy, leaving the audience with that sense of eager anticipation.

Snow Day!
by Lester Laminack

Tone
The overall tone of this read aloud is light, fun.

Intensity
Energy begins high and remains high.

Pacing
Overall, the pace of this read aloud is rather steady. It moves at a quick clip that reflects the high energy of the text.

Mood
The general mood of this book is eager anticipation, leaving the reader with a positive, upbeat feeling.

READ-ALOUD TUTORIAL 5

Polar Bears by Gail Gibbons

By now you may be wondering how this might be different with a nonfiction text. Let's take a look at *Polar Bears* by Gail Gibbons. The first thing I notice with this book is the author's name. I have come to trust Gail Gibbons to deliver a detailed, factual presentation of information in a concise and accessible style. True to form, when I open this book I find large illustrations that are realistic (not like photographs, but not animated or cartoon-like, either). A quick look through the book reveals the use of captions and labels with many of the illustrations. Take a moment to read the text on any page where these captions or labels are included in the art, and you find that they illuminate the information or expand the role of the text. In short, this book is meant to teach us something about polar bears. It isn't a story about a polar bear's day or a story in which a polar bear is a character. Instead, it is solid information.

When I step into an information book, my mind turns on the voice of the Discovery Channel narrators. I hear that careful and deliberate pace that avoids rushing an idea. I hear the clear and articulate voice enunciating carefully with a focus on the information over all else. I hear the timbre of a voice of authority, a voice I should trust. And as I open a Gail Gibbons book I hear that same voice. The tone is more formal and serious, suggesting an intensity that is powerful yet restrained, with a pace that is careful and deliberate, pausing intentionally in places for my mind to catch up with the flow of the information.

The snow blows, the wind howls. The temperature is very cold, hovering around −30 degrees Fahrenheit (−34 degrees Celsius). Through the snowy scene a great white bear appears, the polar bear.

Let's take a closer look at the opening page:

> **The snow blows, the wind howls. The temperature is very cold, hovering around –30 degrees Fahrenheit (–34 degrees Celsius).**
>
> **Through the snowy scene a great white bear appears, the polar bear.**

Can't you hear that voice? Hold that voice in your head and read through these opening lines. Here's what I hear:

"The snow blows,	[Pause and hold the *s* on *blows* for a second.]
The wind	[Place a slight emphasis on the *d* in *wind* creating the slightest pause.]
howls.	[Full stop.]
The temperature is very	[Emphasis on *very*.]
cold,	[Slight emphasis on the *d* in *cold*, creating a very slight pause.]
hovering around –30 degrees Fahrenheit	[Pause here and drop your voice before proceeding.]
(–34 degrees Celsius).	[The lower voice suggest an aside, like saying "in other words."]
Through the snowy scene	[Carefully enunciate these two words—*snowy/scene*.]
a great white bear	[Place a slight emphasis on these words—*great/white/bear*.]
appears,	[Pause and alter the intensity as if you are announcing the arrival of someone.]
the polar bear.	

Let's take a look at another small sample and notice how control of pacing and intensity can help call attention to vocabulary. In this passage, the word *tundra* is defined by the words preceding it:

> **The polar bear lives in the Arctic, the area that surrounds the North Pole. Part of the Arctic is frozen, treeless land called tundra. Most of the Arctic is ocean. Ice covers the water most of the year.**

In some of the fiction we examined earlier, we took signals for pacing and intensity from the placement of words on the page and/or from the use of white spaces. In this book and many nonfiction books we find a more typical paragraph structure, which provides no signals about pacing or intensity. So

---

Polar Bears
by Gail Gibbons

Tone

The overall tone of this read aloud is sober, solemn and focused.

Intensity

The energy of this text is steady, controlled and should front the information over the presentation

Pacing

The general pace of this read aloud is rather consistent. There are a few places where the pace would slow a bit to give the listeners time to process the information.

Mood

The general mood of this read aloud is serious, informative.

Read-Aloud Tutorial

we take our cues from the language and the layering of ideas. Let's play with pacing and intensity here and find out how they can influence the power of the language. Read the three sentences above and try to keep your pace steady, in a low, quiet volume. Now try that aloud one or two times. Notice how doing so has you move right over the word *tundra* and how the definition could get lost by the time you reach the end of the fourth sentence.

Notice that these four sentences are focused on the habitat of polar bears. The four sentences are building that one big idea, yet that one big idea is made up of these six smaller ideas:

1. Polar bears live in the Arctic.

2. The Arctic is the area surrounding the North Pole.

3. Part of the Arctic is frozen, treeless land.

4. That frozen, treeless land is called tundra.

5. Most of the Arctic is ocean.

6. Ice covers the water most of the year.

Now try it again with that Discovery Channel narrator voice in your head. Think about how we placed emphasis on key words and particular sounds to draw attention to those ideas. Think about how we paused in targeted places to give the mind a chance to layer in the ideas that are building across the sentences. Try reading aloud with attention to pacing and intensity that will help the audience layer the six smaller ideas to gain insight into the one big idea.

Let's take one sentence from the four: "Part of the Arctic is frozen, treeless land called tundra." Note how the sentence embeds a definition for new vocabulary (*tundra*). To read this too quickly would likely result in the audience whizzing right past that connection. And they are just as likely to miss the notion that only *part* of the Arctic is tundra. So let's try to control pacing and intensity in a way that would call attention to those two ideas.

"**Part**	[Place emphasis on this word.]
of the Arctic,	[Slight pause.]
is frozen, treeless land	[Slight pause.]
called tundra."	[Emphasize the word *tundra*.]

Do you hear a difference this way? The shift in intensity to stress the words *part* and *tundra* calls attention to them, gives them weight. The pauses or attention to pacing help the listener layer information and build meaning. The simple act of attending to tone, intensity, pacing, and mood can make every read aloud more robust.

Stepping Back to Consider Our Intentions

When you next launch a read-aloud experience in your classroom, think about your intentions. Are you reading aloud to *inspire* your students to become readers and writers? Are you trying to have them fall in love with a genre, topic, title, author, or illustrator? Or is the experience an *investment* in the development of their language and understandings? Are you building background for future instruction? Or will you be reading aloud to them at the point of *instruction*? Will you select the text you read for the purpose of teaching them something? Will this text build off the previous ones? Will it be grounded in a unit of study in a subject area?

Whatever your intentions when you next read aloud, think about setting the stage to maximize the effect. Our students thrive on structure and routine, so the read-aloud experience should be a consistent event. You can find very specific suggestions for six opportunities for reading aloud across a single day in *Learning Under the Influence of Language and Literature* (Laminack & Wadsworth, 2006). In that book, Reba Wadsworth and I suggest six different times in the typical school day when teachers could insert a read aloud. In addition, we offer a very specific purpose for each of them. You will also find more than 400 picture books listed out, annotated, and organized by purpose. Having a designated time and purpose is important. It is also important to set the stage in other ways.

- Physical setting—have a consistent location from which you will read. If the audience is seated in chairs, I like sitting on a tall stool while reading aloud. Otherwise, I prefer to sit on the floor, with my audience gathered close enough to see the illustrations.

- Select a location that makes the book visible without having the glare of a window behind you, and avoid sitting

What the Research Says

The critical role of reading widely at increasingly more challenging levels cannot be overemphasized. Many parents, administrators, and teachers still believe that literacy is primarily a matter of skill instruction. The importance of practicing, using, and "living" literacy is often overlooked. Perhaps this is partly because we live in a society that does not always practice the literacy it preaches and supposedly values—libraries are underfunded, television is the predominant source of entertainment and information, and 70 percent of all reading is done by only 10 percent of the population (Sanders, 1994; Shefelbine, 2004).

in a position that causes the audience to have to look up the entire time.

- Establish an atmosphere in the classroom that supports engagement in the read-aloud experience. Clear other materials and work away. Make yourself and the text the focal point. Eliminate distractions or reduce them to a minimum.

- Introduce the text you are presenting in the read aloud—show the cover and announce the title, author, and illustrator. Invite the students to examine the cover art. Read the flap copy regarding the text and the brief profile of the author and illustrator. Read the dedication. Examine the endpapers and do a brief picture walk through the book if it is a picture book. Lead the students to use the information garnered to make predictions about the text.

- Introduce the read-aloud experience by stating your purpose: "Today as I read I'd like you to be thinking about...," or "I selected this text for read aloud today because it will help us understand what was going on during the days when Anne Frank was a little girl...."

- Introduce essential vocabulary if you know there are words that are likely to cause confusion and will not be developed through the context. Call attention to the terms and give a brief explanation up front. Then, as you read, simply pause and remind students of the word. Keep reading.

- If your intentions for the read-aloud experience warrant it, draw attention to specific features of the text, such as text boxes, charts, sidebars, graphs, captions, labels, bold type, font type shifts, font size shifts, diagrams, the index, appendices, and so on.

- If your intentions warrant it, pause at critical junctures to raise questions in students' minds.

Lester's Favorite (at the Moment) Read Alouds

I love reading aloud for kids (and adults). I find pleasure in discovering another wonderful book that will be a hit as a read aloud and then playing with it until I have the performance ready. I have my standard read-aloud books that I count on time and time again. I have books that I have used in read-aloud experiences or performances for years. If you love reading aloud, if you fall into the book and live there for a few moments and become part of the whole experience, then you know what I mean. I'm guessing you have your favorites, too. Well, just imagine the list we could amass if we began sharing our lists of standards. I'll go first.

All the Places to Love by Patricia MacLachlan

I adore the lush, fluid river of language flowing through the writing of Patricia MacLachlan. This is my favorite of her many books. I love the gentle rhythm, the soft, tender feelings of love and respect this narrator has for his family.

The Barn Owls by Tony Johnston

Tony Johnston is a writer whose work I have long admired. Of all her many books this is one of my two favorites. It is a sensory feast with attention to small details used to build a sense of the cycle of life, and it has a respect for nature, traditions, and place. I love reading this one aloud. It drips slowly off the tongue like raindrops from leaves.

Bat Loves the Night by Nicola Davies

The narrative flow of one day in the life of a bat revealed in layers of gentle poetic prose makes this a delight to read aloud. It slowly develops vocabulary and helps build a baseline of information for deeper questions and further investigation.

Come a Tide by George Ella Lyon

George Ella has an exquisite ear for capturing the language of the people of rural Appalachia. This story gives us an opportunity to listen to the music of that language and to deepen our understanding of the bonds of family and neighbors in life of a bygone era.

In November by Cynthia Rylant

I love the beautiful descriptions, the sensory detail, the music of this book. It aptly captures the warmth and love of friends and family gathering in this special time of year. I count on Cynthia Rylant to capture the people, the language, and the sense of place when she writes of home.

Koala Lou by Mem Fox

Long ago, Mem Fox stole my heart. I fell in love with her words. She is a master of rhythm and queen of big messages in small packages. I adore this book because the read aloud is like music and the message is tuned to my heart.

Mississippi by Diane Seibert

Beautiful nonfiction told in a long poem written from the perspective of the river itself. Diane Seibert has the ability to let landforms, regions, and rivers speak to us, to tell us their own story. She teaches us and entrances us all at the same time.

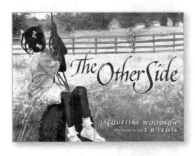

The Other Side by Jacqueline Woodson

Jacqueline Woodson is one of those writers who is willing to take on the tough issues in the lives of children. She consistently does it with grace and eloquence. I love how this book captures the innocence of children, their open minds and accepting hearts, even when the adults around them are frozen by fear and distrust that breeds hatred. The rhythm and flow of this one makes it a pleasure to share as a read aloud.

Saturdays and Teacakes by Lester Laminack

My own memoir, and I think my best writing thus far. I love reading this aloud because I know the music by heart in this tribute to my maternal grandmother. A book holds the potential to take you into the life of the author and the life of the reader all at once. I aimed for that in this book.

Scarecrow by Cynthia Rylant

I love the use of repeated lines, building up and layering meaning, giving life and emotion to a common scarecrow with such attention to small details that matter. Exquisite. A wonderful, slow-paced feast for the reader and the listener.

Seven Blind Mice by Ed Young

This is a favorite because it has the potential to mean more and more each time you visit. It has a nice storytelling quality with parallel details that layer over the story. I adore the play on color, and seeing in part, and the gender twist with White Mouse. It is one to read over and over as you "discover" newer and deeper meanings.

Twilight Comes Twice by Ralph Fletcher

Ralph captures the magic of dawn and dusk in exquisite language. This books reads like a long poem and is peppered with metaphor and luscious description.

Water Dance by Thomas Locker

I love reading this beautiful presentation of art. Locker's paintings are simply impeccable, and the writing here is art as well. I especially enjoy the water talking directly to the reader, identifying itself in all the forms water can take on its journey. It is poetry and music to read aloud.

What You Know First by Patricia MacLachlan

Patricia MacLachlan is one of my five favorite writers. I love her writing. It is a feast to read aloud, to listen to. This particular piece has beautiful repetitions and parallel structures that I adore. I never rush this one—as if I were enjoying a rich, expensive dark chocolate truffle. I relish every moment.

Wilfrid Gordon McDonald Partridge by Mem Fox

I fell in love with Mem because of this book. It was one of the first books I read aloud so frequently that people actually brought it to me and asked that I sign their copy. I had to smile and say, I didn't write it, I just love it. I adore the tenderness, the love, and the innocence of a child captured here. I love the movement through the book, taking Wilfrid from person to person in search of understanding to help his dear friend. I love the opportunity to play with voices. I simply love this book and I adore Mem—so would you expect less?

Wilfrid Gordon McDonald Partridge
Written by Mem Fox   Illustrated by Julie Vivas

Yo! Yes? by Chris Raschka

What a delight to read aloud. You actually get to be two personalities when you read this one aloud. I have actually stood in two chairs and moved from one to the other as I shift between these two characters. (Don't look at me like that—try it!)

And a Few More on the Playful Side:

Bubba and Beau Go Night-Night by Kathy Appelt

Oh my, how I love to read this book (and the other two Bubba and Beau books as well). It is such fun to step into the persona, pull out the accent from my repertoire of voices, and just cut loose.

Diary of a Worm by Doreen Cronin

I have three favorite scenes in this book. I have read it thousands of times (literally) to thousands of people (literally). I still laugh when I read my three favorite entries. This one is an opportunity to fine-tune the importance of pace and intensity and tone. Have fun with it.

Epossumondas by Coleen Salley

I love Coleen. I love the music of her New Orleans–flavored voice. I love the personality that she exudes, and I try to capture the essence of that when I read this one aloud. I listen for Miss Coleen's pacing and slow down. I exaggerate and stretch words where I have heard her do it and take a few liberties of my own. I tap into my own rural Southern roots when I bring these words off the page.

Hungry Hen by Richard Waring

This one is a wonderful opportunity to explore the impact of pacing. Read this too quickly and you fail to allow the reader to build up the suspense, to anticipate and take delight in being right or being shocked by the unexpected ending.

My Lucky Day by Keiko Kasza

The voice in this book is a treat to play with. Choose a voice for the piglet, who is feigning shock. Choose another for the fox, who is delighted to find dinner knocking at his door. Let your voice tease the listeners as they try to decide whose day is lucky.

The Recess Queen by Alexis O'Neill

Get an attitude. Let it rip. This book features a playground bully who meets her match in a teeny-tiny kid who is too new to understand the rules. Let your voice carry that attitude out to your listeners. Then everyone is surprised by the outcome.

Roller Coaster by Marla Frazee

Roller Coaster is a tight text capturing a moment in a big day at an amusement park. The focus of the book is on confronting the fears that come with a first ride on the roller coaster. The craft in the writing offers opportunities for the reader to play with pacing and intensity to build the tension associated with this event. Have fun when you read it.

Snow Day! by Lester Laminack

Yeah, I know, I wrote it and this looks like shameless self-promotion. But I love reading this one aloud. I crafted it to be a one-sided conversation where the narrator is speaking directly to you. I made decisions regarding line breaks, font changes, and punctuation to create the breathless energy of hoping for a snow day and frantically searching for all the essentials to make it great. The energy in the read aloud should build, layering the imagination with greater and greater anticipation. And the ending should bring a smile.

Tanka Tanka Skunk! by Steve Webb

OK, this is all about rhythm. Read it aloud a few times to find that beat, then try to read it with a few body movements. This can become a class favorite, so jump in there and let it rip.

The Three Armadillies Tuff by Jackie Mims Hopkins

So if you know me at all, if you have heard me read a few books aloud, you know that I can be a bit of a ham—just a tiny bit. Well, this book is a stage for a ham. There are four great characters in the three sisters and the coyote. You'll have a wonderful time cutting loose and stepping into the four personalities. When I read this I usually hear, "Read it again!"

TEACHING TUTORIAL 4

My Favorite Ways to Introduce a Book

1. Picture Walk
2. Book Talk/Commercial
3. Author Profile
4. Theme/Topic Link
5. Just Start Reading

Picture Walk

Today we are going to read this book [hold the book so the front cover is visible]. It is called *Snow Day!* The author is Lester Laminack, and the illustrator is Adam Gustavson. Take a look at the illustration on the front. These two kids seem to be zipping down a hill on this red sled. Before we read this one, let's take a walk through the pictures and see what is going on. Turn to the first illustration and begin a conversation. It may go something like this: Well, I see a boy looking right at us and his eyes are really large. He looks excited. I wonder what he might be excited about? And look at the girl lying there on the floor in front of the TV. Mmmm, that's interesting, the man on the TV is standing in front of a map and that looks like clouds and snowflakes. I wonder what that man is talking about. Oh look, there is one more person in the illustration. See the man over here? He looks like a grown-up and he's wearing an apron and has a spatula in his hand. It looks as if he is coming from the kitchen to see what is going on. Now I'm really wondering what these three are talking about. Let's turn the page and take a look at the next illustration, shall we?

Book Talk/Commercial

Just imagine how excited you'd feel if you heard the TV weatherperson announce the possibility of a big snowfall on a *SCHOOL NIGHT!* Imagine what you'd be thinking about and how excited you would get. Perhaps you'd be thinking about staying up late to watch TV. Or sleeping in the next morning. Or you might be thinking about your homework and how you could just skip it until the next day. Maybe you'd be thinking about all the fun you could have spending the day playing in the snow—snow forts and snowball fights, sledding and snowmen.... Oh, and then you'd need to come inside and get warm. There's bound to be hot chocolate on a snow day—mmmm, I do love a good mug full of hot chocolate. Today we are reading *Snow Day!* I can hardly wait, let's get right to it and see what happens on this snow day....

Author Profile

Today I have a new book for us. This one is called *Snow Day!*, and look, it's written by Lester Laminack. We know who that is. He wrote *Saturdays and Teacakes*. Do you remember seeing and hearing him read that book on the DVD I have? He also wrote a few other books that we have in our room; do you remember which books he wrote? Let's take a look [have the books close by and hold each one up]. He wrote *Jake's 100th Day of School* and *Trevor's Wiggly-Wobbly Tooth*. Those stories remind us of the things we do at school. We have talked about that several times. He also wrote *The Sunsets of Miss Olivia Wiggins*; remember how that one always makes me cry because it reminds me of my grandmother? I checked Lester's Web site and bookmarked the page for you if you'd like to go there for yourself. I discovered that Lester was a teacher in an elementary school and in a university. That helps us understand why he might write about what happens at school in *Trevor's Wiggly-Wobbly Tooth* and *Jake's 100th Day of School*. I'm thinking *Snow Day!* might have a connection to school as well. Let's try to remember to look for that as we read. I also found out that he grew up in a very small Alabama town called Heflin. And I discovered that *Saturdays and Teacakes* is a memoir about growing up in that small town. I am wondering if there is anything from his life in this new book, *Snow Day!* Let's think about that when we are listening. Remind me to check the dedication, since authors sometimes share connections for us there. And one more thing I discovered when reading about Lester. He lives in Asheville, North

Carolina, and it does snow there in winter. So now I'm wondering if that's where he got the idea for this new book. Let's take a look inside and see what we find.

Theme/Topic Link

Sometimes unexpected things can make us change our plans. Rainstorms can cause us to cancel soccer practice. A flat tire on a bike can make us walk when we planned to ride. Sometimes we expect something in the mail and it takes a week longer to arrive than we thought it would. A delay at the airport can cause us to miss a trip. Unexpected events can make us change our plans, and that is what we are reading about this week. I have a basket of books here, and we will read one each day. These are stories about all kinds of plans that just don't work out because something unexpected happens. Let's take a look at the first one, *Snow Day!*, written by Lester Laminack, with illustrations by Adam Gustavson. Take a moment before we begin to read; let's think about what unexpected event may make these characters change their plans. What plans do you suppose they had? [At this point I sometimes have students share their thinking with someone near first, then share out.] Let's settle in and see what goes awry in this story....

Just Start Reading

Well, duh... this is pretty clear, huh? All kidding aside, I often just share the title, author, and illustrator, then begin.

Closing Comments and a Final Plea

What the Research Says

We should provide all children, regardless of their achievement levels, with as many reading experiences as possible. Indeed, this becomes doubly imperative for precisely those children whose verbal abilities are most in need of bolstering, for it is the very act of reading that can build those capacities. An encouraging message for teachers of low-achieving students is implicit here. We often despair of changing our students' abilities, but there is at least one partially malleable habit that will itself develop abilities—reading (Cunningham & Stanovich, 1998)!

Reading aloud to the children in our lives seems like such a commonsense practice. Yet in recent years I have heard teachers remark that they simply don't have time to read aloud. These same teachers comment on how much they enjoy reading to their students and share fond memories from their own school years when teachers read to them. It is as if we feel the need to justify the use of precious time to read aloud. We seem afraid to exercise our own good judgment to do what our professional knowledge tells us is right and good for children. Let me remind you that we *are* professionals. Somehow in the midst of all the demands for higher scores, the very real threats of school takeovers, and the infiltration of scripted programs, we have lost sense of this fact. We *are* professionals.

Remember that we have a specific knowledge base that sets us apart from the rest of the population. We have deep understandings and insights into human growth and development, language and literacy development, pedagogy, curriculum design, and instructional technique. We *know* things the general public simply doesn't understand. Yet we continue to allow influences beyond our profession diminish our sense of self and steal our very professional identity from us, and in doing so we lose our professional integrity.

I urge you to renew that knowledge base. Revisit those books and articles that once sparked your professional knowledge and piqued your curiosity. Revisit those books and articles, conference proceedings, and videos that once excited you, invigorated you, and nudged you into new practices in your classroom. Revisit the last time you felt charged and in charge. Remember those days when you entered the profession, and remember the feelings and beliefs that brought you in.

I can't know your reasons for becoming a teacher, but I am virtually certain that there is not one teacher breathing who chose this profession because he or she wanted to raise a test score or make adequate yearly progress goals for the school. Whatever the reason you had for becoming a teacher, I'm confident it had something to do with children and their welfare and their sense of self. I am fairly confident it had something to do with helping children reach their potential and realize their dreams. Let's refocus our energies on the children. Let's make each decision based on what we believe would be good for the specific children in our charge. Let's make daily decisions with that in mind. Let's trust our professional judgment to guide our decisions. Let's teach with integrity and know that our students will do well if our attention is directed toward the child—the mathematician and scientist and artist and writer and musician and athlete and reader and social scientist and dreamer and inventor and visionary in each of them. Let's teach children again. Let's be reminded we are here to raise *humans*, not scores.

Let me remind you that literature in all its many forms has such potential to expand the horizons of every child—regardless of background or baggage, privilege or poverty. When we read aloud to them, we offer them new vistas and new visions. We offer them new ways of coping with life's issues and pleasures. We offer them new opportunities to grow their language and their understandings. We help them realize how much there is to learn. When we read aloud, we show them how we gain a little knowledge to ask better questions, and that asking better questions drives us to read even more. When we read aloud, we introduce them to people just like them and like no one they have ever imagined. We help them realize their homes are only a small sample of the dwellings of all humanity. We help them realize their families are one of many ways families can be formed. We help them realize that the sound of their language is one note in the music of the many languages on the globe. When we read aloud, we help them realize what they value and cherish as worthy and worthwhile and holy is only one way of assigning importance in this great big world. When we read aloud, we help them realize that no matter who we are, no matter where we live, no matter what we value, no matter how we sound, we are more alike as human beings from the inside out than we are different from the outside in. But perhaps the most important message that comes from our reading aloud to them is one that says *you* are worth the time this will take. *You* are the focus of what I do as a teacher. When I read to you, I give you that same undivided attention you once had snuggling in the lap of a caregiver who read to you. When a teacher reads aloud, it is a bonding between the teacher, the children, the books, and the act of reading. That in itself is worthy.

Friends, I urge you to reconnect to those stirrings that brought you into this profession. I urge you to refocus your attention to the children in your care. There is no more precious treasure on this globe than the children of its people. Nothing holds greater potential for good, for truth, for justice than the children on this Earth. We cannot afford to contaminate that precious resource with notions of worth connected to the number on a test. We cannot afford to lead our children to the belief that our school's success, our success, their success, and, by association, their worth, is invested in adequate yearly progress. For a child to believe that he or she has responsibility for the success of a school, a community, a state, and the nation is ludicrous at best and immoral at worst.

Take some time now to search through your books, to carefully and critically examine your schedule, to revisit your vision about why this matters. Pull a favorite book, stop what you are doing, and read to them.

In all things, be kind and truthful. Let nothing you do take from a child his or her dignity as a human being, his or her integrity as a learner, his or her identity as one who is capable. Cause no intentional harm.

Peace be with you,
Lester

References

Professional Books

Beck, I. L., & McKeown, M. G. (2001). Text talk: Capturing the benefits of read-aloud experiences for young children. *The Reading Teacher, 55*(1), 10–20.

Cambourne, B. (1988). *The whole story.* New York: Scholastic.

Cochran-Smith, M. (1984). *The making of a reader.* New York: Ablex Publishing.

Cunningham, A. E., & Stanovich, K. E. (1998). What reading does for the mind. *American Educator, 22*(1–2), 8–15.

Fox, M. (1993). *Radical reflections.* San Diego, CA: Harcourt.

Fox, M. (2001). *Reading magic.* San Diego, CA: Harcourt.

Halliday, M. A. K. (1973). *Explorations in the functions of language.* London: Edward Arnold.

Heath, S. B. (1983). *Ways with words: Language, life, and work in communities and classrooms.* Cambridge, England: Cambridge University Press.

Laminack, L. L., & Wadsworth, R. M. (2006). *Reading aloud across the curriculum.* Portsmouth, NH: Heinemann.

Laminack, L. L., & Wadsworth, R. M. (2006). *Learning under the influence of language and literature.* Portsmouth, NH: Heinemann.

Sanders, B. (1994). *A is for ox: The collapse of literacy and the rise of violence in an electronic age.* New York: Vintage Books.

Shefelbine, J., & Newman, K. K. (2004). *Sipps challenge assessment record book.* Oakland, CA: Developmental Studies Center.

Smith, F. (1998). *The book of learning and forgetting.* New York: Teachers College Press.

Snow, C. E. (1983). Literacy and language: Relationships during the preschool years. *Harvard Educational Review, 53*(2), 165–189.

Snow, C. E., Tabors, P. O., Nicholson, P., & Kurland, B. (1995). SHELL: Oral language and early literacy skills in kindergarten and first-grade children. *Journal of Research in Childhood Education, 10*, 37–48.

Snow, C. E., & Dickinson, D. K. (1991). Some skills that aren't basic in a new conception of literacy. In E. M. Jennings & A. C. Purves (Eds.), *Literate systems and individual lives: Perspectives on literacy and schooling* (pp. 175–213). Albany, NY: SUNY Press.

Stanovich, K. E., & Cunningham, A. E. (1993). Where does knowledge come from? Specific associations between print exposure and information acquisition. *Journal of Educational Psychology, 85*(2), 211–229.

Children's Books

Ada, A. F. (2001). *Yours truly, Goldilocks.* New York: Aladdin.

Ada, A. F. (2004). *With love, Little Red Hen.* New York: Aladdin.

Ada, A. F. (2006). *Dear Peter Rabbit.* New York: Aladdin.

Appelt, K. (2003). *Bubba and Beau go night-night.* Orlando, FL: Harcourt Children's Books.

Bell-Rehwoldt, S. (2007). *You think it's easy being the tooth fairy?* San Francisco: Chronicle Books.

Cronin, D. (2003). *Diary of a worm.* New York: Joanna Cotler Books.

Davies, N. (2004). *Bat loves the night.* Cambridge, MA: Candlewick.

Dahl, R. (1998). *The BFG.* New York: Puffin.

Fletcher, R. (1997). *Twilight comes twice.* New York: Clarion Books.

Fox, M. (1985). *Wilfrid Gordon McDonald Partridge.* La Jolla, CA: Kane/Miller Book Publishers.

Fox, M. (1988). *Koala Lou.* Orlando, FL: Harcourt Children's Books.

Frazee, M. (2003). *Roller coaster.* San Diego, CA: Harcourt.

Gibbons, G. (2002). *Polar bears.* New York: Holiday House.

Gibbons, G. (2007). *Snakes.* New York: Holiday House.

Hopkins, J. M. (2002). *The three armadillies Tuff.* Atlanta: Peachtree.

Johnston, T. (2000). *The barn owls.* Somersworth, MA: Charlesbridge Publishing.

Kasza, K. (2003). *My lucky day.* New York: Putnam Juvenile.

Keats, E. J. (1998). *A letter to Amy.* New York: Puffin.

Laminack, L. L. (2004). *Saturdays and teacakes.* Atlanta: Peachtree.

Laminack, L. L. (2007). *Snow day!* Atlanta: Peachtree.

Lester, H. (2002). *Hooway for Wodney Wat.* Boston: Walter Lorraine Books.

Locker, T. (1997). *Water dance.* Orlando, FL: Harcourt Children's Books.

Lovell, P. (2001). *Stand tall, Molly Lou Melon.* New York: Putnam.

Lyon, G. E. (1990). *Come a tide.* New York: Orchard Paperbacks.

MacLachlan, P. (1994). *All the places to love.* New York: HarperCollins.

MacLachlan, P. (1998). *What you know first.* New York: HarperTrophy.

McLerran, A. (2004). *Roxaboxen.* New York: HarperTrophy.

O'Neill, A. (2002). *The recess queen.* New York: Scholastic.

Rankin, L. (1996). *The handmade alphabet.* New York: Puffin.

Raschka, C. (1993). *Yo! Yes?* New York: Scholastic.

Reynolds, P. H. (2004). *Ish.* Cambridge, MA: Candlewick.

Rylant, C. (1998). *Scarecrow.* Orlando, FL: Harcourt Children's Books.

Rylant, C. (2000). *In November.* Orlando, FL: Harcourt Children's Books.

Salley, C. (2002). *Epossumondas.* Orlando, FL: Harcourt Children's Books.

Siebert, D. (2001). *Mississippi.* New York: HarperCollins.

Waring, R. (2001). *Hungry hen.* New York: HarperCollins.

Webb, S. (2004). *Tanka tanka skunk!* London: Orchard Books.

Woodson, J. (2001). *The other side.* New York: Putnam Juvenile.

Young, E. (1992). *Seven blind mice.* New York: Philomel.